Lean Thinking for Emerging Healthcare Leaders

Lean Thinking for Emerging Healthcare Leaders

How to Develop Yourself and Implement Process Improvements

Arnout Orelio

BUSINESS EXPERT PRESS

Leader in applied, concise business books

Mensen beter maken in de praktijk (2020)
Mensen beter maken (2019); English edition: *Lean Thinking in Healthcare* (2021)
Stili Novi Publishing
Dorstige Hartsteeg 1c
3512 NV Utrecht
The Netherlands
www.stilinovi.com

First published in 2020 by
Business Expert Press, LLC
222 East 46th Street, New York, NY 10017
www.businessexpertpress.com

ISBN-13: 978-1-95253-830-8 (paperback)
ISBN-13: 978-1-95253-831-5 (e-book)

Business Expert Press Healthcare Management Collection

Collection ISSN: 2333-8601 (print)
Collection ISSN: 2333-861X (electronic)

First edition: 2020

10 9 8 7 6 5 4 3 2 1

Printed in the United States of America.

Abstract

Lean Thinking for Emerging Healthcare Leaders: How to Develop Yourself and Implement Process Improvements, aims at solving the issues in modern day healthcare by handing over the reins of the improvement process to healthcare professionals themselves. Putting those who are doing the work and are closest to the actual situation in the lead. The purpose of this book is to help healthcare leaders who want to be of value to their colleagues and patients.

This book educates you, as a medical professional, in the core theories and concepts of the art and science of Lean leadership and management. It will teach you how to improve healthcare from the inside, making it safer, better, faster, more accessible, and more affordable.

Most importantly the book will help to understand how to develop yourself and your leadership in such a way that will best benefit your patients. This includes change management practices that will help to build commitment with your co-workers, management, patients, and other stakeholders.

With this book we want to inspire, motivate, and stimulate you to lead continuous improvement—while being respectful to people—on the way to ideal care for every patient.

The primary target audience for the book are medical professionals who have recently acquired leadership, management, or business responsibilities. Think of physicians, nurses, dentists, pharmacists, or other medical professionals who have recently been promoted to the management ranks of healthcare or started their own businesses. The book will also be of high value to those who (recently) obtained leadership positions—having no hierarchical power—like project leaders, problem solvers, change managers, and innovators. Because most of the teachings in the book are meta skills and ways of thinking the book is easily relatable and transferable to other disciplines and even sectors.

Keywords

lean thinking; leadership; healthcare; hospital; team; organization; management; healthcare management; healthcare leadership; lean leadership; lean management; medical leadership; personal development; process improvement; results; safer; better; compassionate; coaching; mentoring; patient centered; lean tools; PDCA; doctors; nurses; medical professionals

Contents

Throughout the book you will find tools you can download, by scanning the corresponding QR code. This QR code will take you directly to the website of the book, leanthinkinginhealthcare.com

SCAN ME

Foreword

Taking care of people is a characteristic motive of healthcare professionals. It goes without saying that *Lean Thinking for Emerging Healthcare Leaders* covers basic explanations on healthcare improvement. The book introduces you to Lean management as a philosophy. Furthermore, Lean is being made clear step by step to be used for methodical and systematic problem solving, improvement of care processes, and innovation. And throughout the book the human aspect of Lean is emphasized over and over again: Being respectful to people.

A lot of attention is rightfully paid to leadership that is required to help facilitate improvement. Not only improvement of care processes and their outcomes but also the important component of helping people develop themselves. This development is as much about the medical professional and leader him (or her) self as it is about fellow care workers and team members.

Arnout Orelio has tons of experience in Lean management in both the manufacturing industry and in healthcare and shares his knowledge and experience in this excellent book.

This book wants to guide you in the process of developing yourself and your leadership in order to improve patient care. It provides structure to learn how you—as a leading professional—can help improve care with great involvement of your fellow care professionals, management, and patients.

Lean Thinking for Emerging Healthcare Leaders guides you—in a practical way—to better, faster, and more accessible care.

Rutger I.F. van der Waal, dermatologist, MD PhD

Introduction

The United States spends more per capita ($8,000 per person) and percentage of GDP per capita (17.4 percent) than any other nation in the world on healthcare. Yet on average the health of the American public is in the lower quadrant of nearly every healthcare quality measure when compared to most of the developed world. Clearly something must be done.

The purpose of this book is to attack the problem from the perspective of the practicing front-line healthcare providers. Most of current attempts to solve this problem are made by administrators instead of providers, which causes two major issues:

1. Administrators have limited knowledge of the actual situation in healthcare systems and processes. Many of them reside in *ivory towers*. This causes their measures for improvement to be ineffective and mostly targeted at the symptoms of bad systems and processes.
2. Administrators do little to engage healthcare providers from the beginning. That's why their measures for improvement have little commitment from those who have to implement them.

What would it be like if we gave the responsibility for improving healthcare to the medical professionals themselves? If those who do the work and who are closest to the actual situation were to be in charge?

Medical Professionals in the Lead

Putting healthcare providers in charge of solving problems in healthcare in order to improve quality and accessibility and reduce costs is certainly not self-evident. But who are better equipped to organize *the right care, at the right time, in the right place*? As a healthcare provider, you know the processes best. As a care provider you are always involved in or responsible for the introduction of new working methods and systems.

If you agree that—as a medical professional—you need to be *in the lead* when it comes to changes, improvements, and innovations in healthcare then the question is "How do you do that?"

For working as a medical professional such as a doctor or a nurse, there are clear paths to what you need to do and learn to become a successful and competent professional. What is striking is that for those medical professionals that want to become leaders there is no such a clear path. What is your responsibility as a leader? What competencies and capabilities do you need? How do you develop those? How do you know whether you are successful as a leader? Here we come across a gap in the education and training of medical professionals in (future) leadership positions.

Existing management culture and training courses on leadership in healthcare often have a corporate and managerial approach to leadership and management. A great deal of energy therefore goes into maintaining the status quo rather than improving and renewing it.

This book takes the ambitions of healthcare leadership up a notch. Not keeping up with your budget but continuous improvement while being respectful to people is your primary responsibility. Your primary tasks as a leader or manager are, therefore, giving direction, managing and improving processes, and developing people to their full potential.

Methodically Improving

In each and every working environment things do go wrong. This includes healthcare. How you deal with these daily problems depends very much on the culture that prevails in your organization. I have noticed in many hospitals that people are focused on solving problems as quickly as possible. A very noble attitude but it often leads to temporary solutions that do not address the source of the problem. In order for the work to continue people work around the problem. In addition, making mistakes is not always accepted. As a result, people tend to solve problems quickly themselves instead of seeking help or discussing the problem with colleagues or patients. All to avoid being blamed and called to account for it. Or even worse to be punished for it!

The result is that although the symptom is treated the problem itself is not solved. You come up with a solution so that you can proceed as quickly as possible. This leads to *workarounds* (working around the problem) and behavior that we often refer to as *firefighting*

It is good to realize that this method of solving problems is very different from the method used by the fire brigade when extinguishing fires. They work very methodically. They assess the situation (the fire) as quickly as possible the primary aim being to get the situation under control. Then they extinguish the fire in a safe and sustainable manner after which they analyze the situation in order to identify the cause and (help) prevent the fire (the problem) from recurring.

What can you learn from this? That in order to solve your daily problems you need a method that helps you to identify problems as quickly as possible, to solve them sustainably, and to learn from them. Just as you methodically diagnose, treat, and provide care for your patients.

Lean Thinking

Methodically and systematically solving problems, improving and innovating requires a philosophy—a set of principles, a way of thinking—which you can hold on to. In this book we use Lean thinking for this.

Lean is the name given at the end of the 1980s to the system Toyota uses to organize its processes. Compared to other automakers they produced high-quality cars with minimal resources, such as inventory and manpower (Womack, Jones, and Roos 1990).

Lean is a word that is associated with the fitness of the body. You could say that Toyota produces "without excessive fat." At the time Lean was believed to be a methodology that you could implement.

It took many years and further study of Toyota to discover that it is a philosophy—a system—based on a set of deeply ingrained values and principles of continuous improvement and respect for people (Liker 2004). It took even more time to discover that Lean leadership is the most important factor in building a Lean system and culture (Liker and Convis 2012).

The essence of the so-called *Toyota Production System* is to make problems visible, to challenge people, and use their creativity to solve problems at the source—in order to eliminate waste—the ultimate goal being the highest quality, the shortest lead time, and the lowest cost (Ohno 1988).

This book provides you as a medical professional with the theories and concepts of Lean leadership and management and is intended to help you improve healthcare itself from the inside.

How This Book Will Help You

The primary target group for the book is medical professionals such as doctors, nurses, dentists, pharmacists, or paramedics who have (recently) been given a managerial position or have started their own businesses. The book will also be of high value to those who (recently) obtained leadership positions—having no hierarchical power—like project leaders, problem solvers, change managers, and innovators.

The book is mainly about the kind of leadership needed to improve processes and develop people. In particular it provides you with *meta skills* and a way of thinking that makes it relatively easy to translate into other disciplines, processes, and even sectors.

Most importantly the book helps you understand how to develop yourself and your leadership in a way that really helps your patients on a daily basis. As a leading professional you will learn how to improve care thereby gaining a high level of commitment from your colleagues, management, patients, and other stakeholders, which results in safer, better, faster, more accessible, and affordable care.

Link to Earlier Work of the Author

In 2019 the author published an earlier work on the subject of Lean thinking in healthcare, in Dutch (Orelio 2019). This earlier work (English title: *Lean Thinking in Healthcare: Safe, Compassionate, Zero Waste, No Struggle*), written on the basis of all his experiences with lean transformations in healthcare, is a hands-on overview of everything needed to build a system and a culture of continuous improvement and respect for people.

This book—a spin-off from his earlier work—focuses on *how to* actually develop yourself, coach others, and improve your processes for the better. It is aimed specifically at healthcare professionals with leadership responsibilities and ambitions. The two books have some overlap, particularly in the first chapters, because these contain the vision, concepts, and theory behind Lean thinking, leadership, and process improvement, in healthcare.[1]

---

[1] Whenever relevant, the first book will be referenced by its English title, to be published in 2021 (Orelio 2021).

CHAPTER 1

Give Direction

Few sectors are as dependent on teamwork as healthcare. Due to the highly specialized healthcare professionals—such as doctors, nurses, lab technicians, physiotherapists, pharmacists—patients sometimes have to deal with as many as 60 care providers during their treatment.

To coordinate the work of all these different people requires intensive collaboration. It is precisely this cooperation and the necessary coordination that is sometimes lacking during care processes. As a result, things easily go wrong especially at the transfer points between the various departments and disciplines. Leadership is needed to shape this collaboration and to let people function as a team. But then what is a team?

A team is a group of people who work together toward a common goal. So, people are not a team because you call them that or you have structured them that way. People are only a team when you give them a common goal.

As a leader your first task is to give direction. By creating a common goal, you connect people with each other, you form a team, and make effective cooperation possible. A common goal gives you something to hold on to when you have to make difficult decisions and gives team members autonomy because they can make decisions without having to meet with all those involved. It is therefore important that you—as a leader—provide direction. But then the question is "Which way do you want to go"?

My vision for healthcare is: *Safely and compassionately, the right care, at the right time, at the right place and no waste or struggle.*

Why Are You Working in Healthcare?

Some people do already in primary school know that they want to become a doctor or a nurse. Others consider it in high school—sometimes at the last minute when they have to choose a university or college to study. Almost all of them want to help people to get well again, help people who are worse off than they themselves are, or words of similar meaning. If you ask healthcare professionals—also the ones in managerial positions—about this almost all of them confirm that the original reason for working in healthcare is to help people and getting them well again.

Rarely (or never?) will you hear someone say: I have always wanted to lead medical professionals from the start. If you ask healthcare professionals, "Why do you think someone takes on a leadership?" many people will answer, "Because they have been asked" or "For status or position" or "For a higher salary." These are all extrinsic motivations. If you ask the leaders themselves about their motivation, they often turn out to be motivated—contrary to expectations—by the urge or need to change things and to improve patient care. The goal for people who choose a leadership position has actually remained the same: they want to help people. However, the way they want to achieve this goal is different.

Staying True to Your Purpose

If you choose or end up in a leading position you will be given new responsibilities and associated tasks and it may seem that other things—such as planning, reporting, and budgets—are more important than helping people. There will be a strong appeal on your sense of responsibility to meet the numbers. Before you know it, you will spend a large part of your time in meetings and at your office reading e-mails and making overviews.

Another risk is that you will work like a headless chicken to help the team or blindly do anything your manager asks you to do. This leads to the well-known firefighting mode, its effect being that you work very hard as a leader but that you achieve little. How very demotivating this can be!

How do you get out of this or—even better—how do you prevent this? First of all, do not lose sight of your original motivation. Regularly ask yourself why you started working in healthcare and why you have chosen a leading position. Then compare it with what you actually do and achieve. Ask yourself: What is the objective here? This question helps you to focus yourself and your team on what is really important. After all, the ultimate goal is to help people and cure them. That hasn't changed. Not even when you started to take the lead. Your role has changed. It is up to you to make sure that the whole team knows what the objectives are and that they have a joint vision of how to achieve those objectives. If you can make this happen you will lead the way. Focus and energy will be the result for you and your team.

Perfection as the Goal[1]

Lean is a philosophy and a system that strives for perfection such as creating the ideal experience for patients. What is the advantage when you take perfection as your goal? Perfection is never feasible, or is it? The latter is one of the reasons to take perfection as a goal. Because in this case there is always something to improve—you will just never be there.

Taking the ideal as a starting point can be very inspiring and motivating because suddenly it becomes clear where you can improve. And if you move in the direction of your ideal this is "automatically" creating a situation that is more enjoyable to work in.

If you strive for perfection then your ultimate goal is the ideal or perfection for all stakeholders (those involved) starting with the patient. Think of 100 percent safe, zero defects, no waste, a 10 for customer satisfaction, and so on. We call this ideal "True North." True North is your long-term goal. True North is like the pole star: unreachable but a very good direction giver. The sharper you define True North the better direction it will give.

You define True North as sharp and unattainable as possible for two reasons. First, for example "zero incidents" is the only goal that you can explain. Just imagine someone in a hospital saying that the goal is to have five medication errors that year. What will people think of that? Only zero is acceptable here. The second reason is that healthcare providers already

---

[1] Orelio 2021, Chapter 1.

have the ambition to deliver perfect work for their patients. So, perfection is your ultimate goal because it requires continuous improvement.

True North is meant as direction giver. But how do you reach this point?

When you formulate an improvement goal or your challenges for the coming years True North helps you to be ambitious and to rise above yourself and make sure that you are moving in the direction of the ideal. True North therefore helps you to see and formulate the challenges for the coming years.

It teaches you to ask yourself in every improvement process, "What is the ideal in this situation?" This then will help you to answer the question, "What should I improve" instead of answering the question, "What can I improve?" This provides focus and direction for yourself, your team, and other stakeholders.

True North for Patients[2]

What would True North mean for a patient? For patients True North means a perfect care process outcome and a perfect experience. You can only realize this structurally when your processes are perfect. A process is perfect when the first time a patient asks for care he is being helped rightly, safely and with compassion and there is no waiting time, no waste, or struggle. "Rightly" means that you do exactly what this patient needs in this situation. This optimal care process is called "one-patient flow" and is the ideal care process. In other words, it is the process you strive for. One-patient flow enables you as a healthcare professional to be fully present while helping your current patient.

An ideal care process implies that you work together as a medical team in such a way that the entire care process runs flawlessly, is providing the right care, at the right time, at the right place for every patient. The starting point for achieving "one-patient-flow" is that every step in the care process provides the right resources at the right time: prevention, diagnosis, treatment, and aftercare. Every step being reliable, predictable, and of value to the patient. Wouldn't that just be great?

---

[2] Orelio 2021, Chapter 1

True North for Your Team[3]

The ideal situation or True North for your team means that team members are 100 percent safe, just like patients are. This does not only mean that you do not get hurt at work but also that you can always share all your problems without any retributions.

In order to help patients to get better, you first have to improve the performance of team members. So, they need to develop themselves. Ideally, they will improve and learn every cycle (i.e., every patient). This applies to everyone, every day, everywhere, that is, there is a culture of continuous improvement and respect for people.

True North for the team implies that you make everyone that is involved better professionals and that the quality of their work increases. Technology is there to support you and not to replace you. The improvement process does not lead to dismissal. You use the freed-up capacity to do more for patients, to add more value. The community your team or organization is part of is also safe, is not being unnecessarily burdened or polluted, and develops through the efforts of your team and organization.

Student's Thoughts

What is your True North? Describe your ideal healthcare team, process, and outcomes from the perspective of your patients in concrete, recognizable, and inspiring terms.

Tip: Make a poster of your True North together with your team and put it up the wall for everyone to see and for people to provide feedback and refer to. This will help you to build focus and prioritize your improvement efforts.

---

[3] Orelio 2021, Chapter 1

CHAPTER 2

The Story of the Boat

Having clarity about which direction you want to go and about what you want to achieve is only the beginning. When you have no plan or strategy your goal will remain just a dream. You will have to develop an approach that ensures that you actually move in the direction of your goal.

You need an improvement strategy. A way to solve the problems that stand in the way of your goals and dreams.

In daily practice you will encounter a wide range of problems. Think of misapprehensions, depleted stock, wrong or incomplete information, complications, and incidents. Practice shows that how you tackle these problems (your improvement strategy) is strongly determined by the way you think. Or as Chris Argyris has formulated, "How you think determines which strategy you actually apply in practice" (Argyris and Schon 1974).

In this chapter you will learn about two different ways of thinking—two different approaches—and their effects. On this basis you can determine which of the two is most likely to get you to your goal. It will help you to make an informed and conscious choice for your improvement strategy and to communicate this to other stakeholders.

Approach one is called the traditional way of improvement. We offer this method because it is the most commonly used one. The vast majority of people in organizations improve and think this way. You will probably recognize it from your own work experience. We present it here to make you aware of the consequences of this approach and of the need to change your strategy. The second approach—clearly a different way of thinking—is what we call *Lean thinking*. This way of thinking is the leitmotif of this book. It is important that you are aware of the consequences of choosing this way of improving. Lean thinking has a profound influence on how you lead and how you support your team in this. By using a metaphor—the story of the boat in the canal—we take you through these two different approaches.

Once Upon a Time There Was . . . a Boat in a Canal . . . [1]

Imagine running a shipping company that owns a boat in a canal. The first question you should ask yourself is, "What is the purpose—the added value—of the shipping company?" Your answer could be, "Transporting parcels and / or passengers from A to B. That's what my customers pay for. That's what they value."

To transport the goods, you have bought exactly the right boat. So now you can start! Or can you ... To make the boat sail it must be able to float. And to be able to float water is needed because of the depth of a boat. The water stands for the resources that an organization needs in

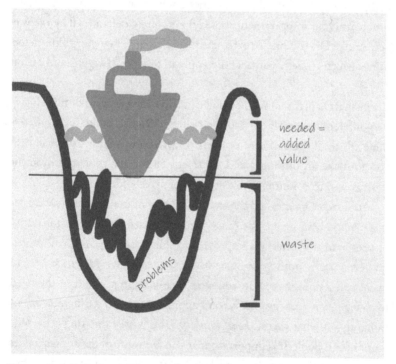

Figure 2.1 Boat in canal: Current condition

---

[1] Orelio 2021, Chapter 2.

the form of people, equipment, buildings, supplies, and so on to do the work. The most important problem to avoid concerning the water is to sail into an obstacle that will cause damage to the boat or that the boat gets stuck.

But how much water does your boat need? The answer is, "Just enough so it will not touch the bottom," meaning it can float freely! In other words, water slightly below the keel. All this water is needed because it makes the boat float and therefore it can sail while not hitting the bottom. You'll never be able to do with less water as long as you're on this boat. All this water—all this capacity (e.g., resources)—is therefore of added value. (See figure 2.1 for an image of the current condition of the boat in the canal.)

In daily practice however an unnecessary amount of water is being used because there is a lot of debris at the bottom. This debris represents the problems you experience in your daily work. You use—waste—extra water to work around these problems and to be able to sail despite these problems.

The Traditional Approach: "Adding Water"

The goal is to sail from A to B and meanwhile not damage or jam the boat. When you don't trust the bottom and are afraid to sail into an obstacle a logical reaction is to sail around it. This means that you have to cover a longer distance. You can also get into further trouble because you might enter a part of the canal that you don't know and a collision might still lie ahead. Of course, this strategy does not provide a solution for the next time a problem occurs or for the next boat that wants to go along the same point in the canal. It is just a workaround and meanwhile the original problem remains.

More far-reaching measures you can take are: to change course, to take a different canal, or even to choose a completely different destination. This all leads to more time and energy needed to get to your destination. This probably means higher costs, disappointed passengers, and late parcels.

What if you would throw in more water? Then the collision will be avoided while not changing course. That's right for that moment. However, the water level will increase and you will not transport more goods

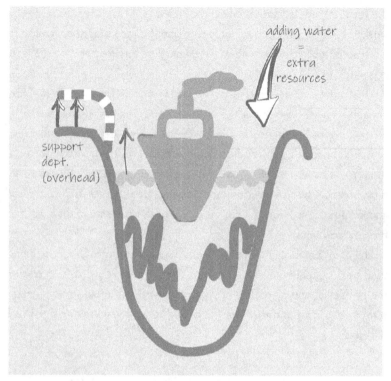

Figure 2.2 Boat in canal: Adding water

or passengers. Thus, you will be spending more money while your income remains the same. Because of the higher water level, it is even more difficult to see what is under water. It also allows the debris to continue to accumulate so that you waste more and more water to "cover" it. (See figure 2.2 for a visualization of what happens if you add water.)

Another consequence is that if the water level rises you also need higher dikes. Higher dikes also need to be widened in order to be stable. In other words, the higher the water level the higher the costs of dikes. Higher dikes also involve greater risks so you have to carry out additional inspections, maintenance, and administration.

In this metaphor the dikes are equal to the "support" departments; in other words, the overhead. All that is necessary to keep the water in the canal. These are for example the personnel and financial administration departments. These higher dikes and their higher risks shift the attention of the management from the boat (the primary process) to the dikes (the support processes) as a result of which they have less and less knowledge about the actual sailing and keeping the boat afloat. This "forces" them to resort to measures such as taking a detour or adding water. A vicious circle is entered in which the costs continue to increase while customers do not receive extra value (services and products) for this.

For the people on the shop floor—in the primary process—this means that they spend more and more time working around the problems. Apart from wasting their time and talents, it has a disastrous impact on their job satisfaction. It is very frustrating to encounter the same problem again and again and to experience that "they"—the managers—do nothing about it.

The Alternative: Lean

In the traditional approach to solving problems people assume that their problems are annoying and they don't want them to come to the surface. The status quo is the starting point. You want as few problems as possible because they show that you are failing and this is bad for your reputation. This results in symptom control, a focus on short-term results and ultimately high costs and frustrations for employees and customers who are the victims of this approach.

In the Lean approach the starting point is long-term benefits for all parties involved. To this end you embrace problems because they give you the opportunity to learn and improve in such a way that you come ever closer to True North—your ultimate goal. You don't solve your problems by adding resources but rather by eliminating your problems so that you need less resources. You can then use the excess resources to do more for your patients.

The first step in the Lean approach is to make a distinction between your work, the resources (water) needed (to let the boat sail), and the waste (all the extra water to cover the debris), the extra resources that you use to deal with problems. You focus your improvement process on "freeing up" resources—in the form of people, equipment, buildings, and supplies. You do this—in our metaphor—by removing the debris in the canal.

It's not easy to remove the debris. Because it is "covered" by the extra water it is difficult to detect. In fact, it seems that you need more instead of less resources because you see people who are working hard and being overburdened, your stock rooms are full, and you are constantly busy arranging things.

You will have to actively search for the debris so that you can see in time whether you are in danger of sailing into an obstacle. When you have a clear image of the debris you can slow down or stop the boat in time. This protects the boat against collisions and gives you the opportunity to examine and remove the debris (the problem). Then you let the boat continue. It is important to focus on the debris that is actually in the way. So, don't start cleaning the entire canal (your entire organization) but focus on the debris you have to remove in order for the boat to continue its journey undamaged. Your focus should only be on the problems that actually stand in the way of your goal—helping patients.

To find out what the debris under water is you have to make it visible. You have to understand exactly what the debris consists of before you can clean up the mess. First you have to have an image of the exact problem before you can take it away. To do this it is necessary to put on goggles and look underwater. As it were you have to learn to look differently first to see the debris under water and the waste of resources that goes with it.

Once you have identified the debris you can clean it up (or have it cleaned up) so that the boat can move on. Then you try to find out why the debris ended up there. In other words, you investigate the root cause of your problem so that you can learn from it and prevent the debris from coming back in the future.

In order to find the root cause of the problem you need to analyze the condition around the problem and start asking yourself, "How did the debris get here?" In other words, "What is the cause of the problem?" You will have to ask as many questions as are needed to get to the root of the problem. Eventually you want to remove the root cause, and you have to solve the problem at the source so that the problem (the debris) will not come back. (See figure 2.3 for a three-step plan for leaders when applying the lean approach to problem solving to the following case.)

Imagine you are in danger of running into an obstacle according to one of your sailors. You stop the boat, put on your diving suit, and together you take a look. You see a bicycle and after some observation and consultation you conclude that the bike is stuck. You call up a technician

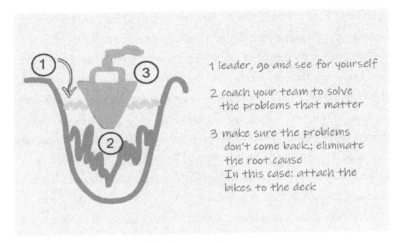

Figure 2.3 Boat in canal: Eliminate the root cause

and together you think of a way to get the bike loose. You hoist the bike out of the water and then the boat can sail again.

Ready! No, because now your most important responsibilities as a leader have to come up. First of all, you ask the technician and the sailor what they have learned from this situation. You use this knowledge to make sure that the next time (read the next bike) the sailor can solve the problem himself because he has the right knowledge, skills, and tools needed on the boat.

Second, you examine the bike and try to figure out how it got into the canal. You'll eventually find out that it fell off another boat. You discuss this with the captain in question and you will make sure that from now on the bicycles will be properly attached to the deck. Then you will share this knowledge with all the other captains who use the canal or also transport bicycles so they can learn from it.

Of course, it may happen that a piece of junk—a problem—is too big for you to (immediately) remove. This is for example the case when the problem costs money to solve, requires special (outside) expertise, or when multiple departments are involved. The problem can also have consequences that you cannot oversee yet. In these cases, you will have to escalate to the next managerial level.

The manager will visit you, assess the situation, and then take a short-term measure: sailing around the obstacle or adding water so that the boat can continue. You need to make sure that this help is immediately available so that the boat doesn't have to stop unnecessarily long. When necessary the manager starts a project to remove the junk.

The essence of the Lean improvement strategy is: The more debris you take away the less water you need. This frees up resources to let larger boats sail, to provide multiple routes or to deliver value in other ways. In other words, you use the resources differently. From wasting time on your problems to delivering added value for your customers: Letting more, faster, or larger boats sail from A to B and other destinations. The scary part of this strategy is that you will keep on lowering the water level to surface problems so there will always be opportunities for self-development and improvement. A Lean leader can never rest on his laurels.

A warning is in place here. When you intend to fire the people, you have freed-up through improvement you will violate the Lean value, "Respect for people." The consequences will be that you lose their trust and people will no longer be willing to help you improve.

New Roles and Responsibilities for Team Members and Leaders

For team members—healthcare professionals on the shop floor—the Lean approach means a major change in behavior but also a relief: Finally, they can (or should) work on the problems they are experiencing on a daily basis instead of working around them and working extra hard to get things done despite these problems. You will have to learn to see "work-arounds" and "troubleshooting" as a waste rather than as work. You have to literally bring the problems to the surface so that you can make them visible to others as well. Then you have to slow down or even stop your process ("the boat") so that you can look at the problem and contain it before matters are getting worse. This is one of the biggest changes and it is counter-intuitive. Especially when in the past people have always been "punished" for stopping the process.

When the process is stopped for too long or if you cannot solve the problem yourself you have to ask for help. As soon as the problem is contained you agree on possible further research and learning and you go back to your work.

As a leader—such as the helmsman and the captain—you will also experience major changes. You have to provide help at the place where the problem occurs (and not from the wheelhouse, the office, or the dikes, the headquarters). You have to make sure that the process (the boat) can continue as soon as possible and then start an analysis of what caused the problem, make sure that everyone learns from the situation, and that the problem does not recur.

You should also make sure that you take other measures—such as adjusting your course—when the problem cannot be solved quickly enough and with the available help. When necessary escalate the situation to senior leadership, the C-suite.

As a leader your most important task is to ensure that the flow improves while not constantly adding water. This is only possible if you regularly go and see for yourself (in the water) what is hindering the flow. This means that you can't just sit in your office or on your computer (from the dikes or the boat) and watch the flow.

For the long term it is important to prevent the canal from silting up again. You will have to keep the process of continuous improvement and learning going. So, you have to continue to make the problems visible. To this end you pay attention to the number of problems that come to light. When there are not enough problems to learn from and improve, then lower the water level so that more problems arise. In turn this offers new opportunities for improvement and thus development for your team and the organization.

Described above is the essence of a Lean management system. Making problems visible, analyze and tackle them thereby developing your people in order to achieve growth. The problems you are looking for are the problems that stand in the way of a smooth passage of the boat. Therefore, your improvement and development processes take place where your patients are not optimally being helped and their care stagnates. Which means that you start where patients do not get the right care at the right time at the right place and experience unsafe situations, waste, or struggles.

Student's Thoughts

1. What is your current approach for improving your processes?
2. If you compare the Lean approach to your current practice what are the differences?
3. What can you do to apply the Lean approach (more often)?
4. What do you expect this to bring you?

CHAPTER 3

Create a Lean Mindset

Once you have determined the direction and established that Lean is indeed the best approach to achieve your goals then your change process can begin. The goal of Lean is that you learn and improve every day in the direction of True North—ideal care for patients. In other words, you solve problems every day and develop yourself and others in a way that continuously improves patient care.

This requires new behavior and a new way of thinking—a different mindset. This mindset is the foundation of your change and ensures that you (yourself) continuously improve while being respectful to people. In this chapter you will learn which mindset—or set of lean principles and values—is at the basis of your improvement process.

Although Lean includes a complete philosophy and system, for an effective change it does not help to try to understand and implement everything all at once. It is better to focus on a small set of essential components as the foundation for your change process.

In this book I limit Lean thinking—the new mindset—to four principles which, applied together, lead to a systematic and sustainable improvement process.

You will then learn to translate these principles into concrete behavior on the basis of three lean leadership skills.

I also make suggestions for how to create this mindset and these skills in yourself and others.

What Is Within Your Control?

You can see your process of improvement—your journey to True North— as a chain of cause–effect relationships. All results (also the bad ones!) start with leadership. This is your input and under your control. All the rest results from this. Through your leadership you influence the mindsets

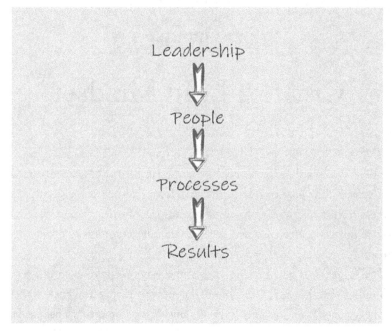

Figure 3.1 From leadership to results

and behaviors of people in your organization. If done rightly they will improve themselves and the processes they work in. These improved processes will give improved results. In Figure 3.1 you find the process that will get you from leadership (your input) to ever better results (the output).

There are entire libraries written about what leadership means and what you can and must do to be successful as a leader. Your team, your colleagues, your managers, and even patients all have expectations about how you are going to behave as a leader. This can be very overwhelming. This is understandable especially if you are just starting your new role as a leader. In order to help you to start off on the right foot you need to focus on what is important and to figure out what works and what does not.

First of all, you share your vision and give direction. If the direction is clear, then it is your job—as a leader—to create a system that makes problems visible. You develop this system on the basis of Lean principles.

The Essence of Lean: The Way of Thinking[1]

The foundation of your Lean system is the way of thinking. If you don't change the way you think you won't achieve a lasting change in behavior and environment. In order to bring focus, we will discuss the four essential components—principles—of Lean thinking:

1. The goal is to be and remain of value to customers (read: patients).
2. People are the source of everything.
3. Continuous improvement is the mantra.
4. Focus on the work place.

Taking these four principles to start with you will move in the right direction and you will be able to come to grips with lasting changes. As your change process progresses you will come across the other principles and parts of the system. Acting in this way you can introduce these principles in phases.

Below we will further elaborate on the four basic principles and provide them with context including some examples of how you can apply these principles in your own work.

The Purpose Is To Be and Remain of Value to Your Patients

The Lean philosophy is focused on the long term. The purpose—your reason for being—is to be of value to others—your customers and society. This means your primary task is to deliver added value in the eyes of your customers—your patients. They determine—their perspective determines—whether what you do is of value. You are adding value when you are solving a concrete problem for people, which they themselves cannot do as safely, well, quickly, or cheaply as you can.

For Lean organizations making money is an "automatic" consequence of the fact that they are of value to other people, making money is not the purpose. When you deliver the right value at the right cost you will make money. This money is needed to be able to invest in growth, changing

---

[1] Orelio 2021, Chapter 5.

patient needs or new ways of being of value. Money is a condition to remain of value in the future.

People Are the Source of Everything

Within the Lean philosophy people are the most important resource and the source of everything. Why is that? First of all because this is close to the purpose of the Lean organization: To provide added value for customers and society. So, your organization is there for other people. Which means that people are important.

The second reason is that only people are able to be creative and therefore can come up with ideas to improve over and over again. People are also the only resource that becomes worth more over time, especially when you invest in them. People who develop themselves will make an increasingly larger more creative contribution to the organization and its customers such as patients. This is the reason why when productivity increases you don't dismiss people but use them to create more value using the newly acquired knowledge and skills.

Continuous Improvement

Lean thinking is about constantly improving. But how do you know whether you are improving? An improvement is a change toward the goal. In other words, a step that makes you move toward True North. By eliminating overload, variation, and waste you retain the ability to do more things of value.

Within the Lean philosophy improvement also means better for all stakeholders. A win–win situation for all parties: patients, family, healthcare professionals, the organization, insurers as well as any other parties involved. This is exactly what you achieve when you eliminate waste and create more value. You are making it better for all parties involved.

Focus on the Workplace

The most important place for someone who thinks Lean is the shop floor or any other workplace where value is added. In fact, it is only relevant to practice continuous improvement when you do it in the workplace. That is the place where it has an impact on your patients and your team.

This focus learns that you cannot create effective improvement by discussing it in a conference room. You have to go to the workplace to find out the truth about the situation you want to improve. So, you want to go to the real place and gather the real information. The workplace can also be an office for example for invoicing, purchasing, or personnel administration.

This focus does not only apply to the physical workplace but also to the people who work there—the healthcare professionals for example. They are the ones who add value. This requires of a leader to show different behavior. You go to the workplace and ask the question, "How are things going?" This is different from opening the door of your office because then the employees have to move toward you. Focus on the workplace means that you go to them, to where the work happens.

Change Your Thinking by Acting Differently

As a Lean leader you want people to think differently. But how do you change people's mindset, their ways of thinking? Contrary to what you might expect not through courses and training but through targeted daily action. John Shook (former CEO of the LEI and Toyota Manager) once said at a Lean conference while talking about changing the culture at the Toyota–General Motors (GM) joint venture known as NUMMI in the 1980s, "It's easier to act your way into a new way of thinking than to think your way into a new way of acting." The insight is that through new routines and ways of working slowly but surely your brain learns new patterns and new ways of thinking.

The advice is to (let people) experiment with the new behavior such as solving problems in a structured way including yourself. Lead the way but don't skip any steps and don't ask for accelerated training. Meaning no shortcuts or condensed training for leaders. Make sure you will be part of the first group that goes through the required training. You have to undergo the same structured training process as your team. This is necessary for learning and applying things in the right way. This ensures that as a leader you literally lead by example. Only when you have mastered the Lean skills and gained sufficient experience you can take on the Lean training and coaching of your team. This requires apart from improvement skills and a problem-solving ability especially leadership skills.

Leadership for Continuous Improvement and Learning[2]

As a Lean leader you make sure that people continuously improve together in a focused way and that they continue to develop themselves. For your leadership this means that it focuses mainly on developing people so that their improvement skills and problem-solving abilities will increase. Even when you are directly involved in solving problems or improving a process you stay focused on the learning process of your team.

As a leader you are mainly a teacher and a coach. You are service-minded; you feel responsible for the success of the employees in the workplace. You must ensure that you set up systems and processes that make deviations visible quickly and easily so that improvement and learning can take place.

What kind of behavior does this require of you as a leader?

The six leadership skills needed for a complete lean transformation of your organization and culture are:

1. Challenge
2. Go where the problem is and watch
3. Ask questions
4. Improve (yourself) continuously
5. Work together, as a team
6. Show respect

Below I work out the three primary lean leadership skills[3] that you can start off with as a (emerging) lean leader.

---

[2] Orelio 2021, Chapter 4.

[3] The selection of these three skills was inspired by a statement of Fujio Cho, former President of Toyota, who said: "Go see, ask why, show respect."

Go Where the Problem is and Watch

The first step in your development as a Lean leader is to go to the workplace to see for yourself what the real condition is. This means that you go to the workplace and examine how things actually stand with your team, the process, and the problems that they experience. It is the only way to make sure that you keep testing your assumptions with the real condition. By doing so you indicate that the work and the wisdom are not with you but with the people who are actually doing the work.

By observing and not being judgmental you will see the real problems and it will become clear which strategy to use to improve. The problems and causes will reveal themselves and this offers an immediate opportunity to involve the team in the analysis and the solutions. When you are not being judgmental there will be room for the facts.

Ask Questions

If my toolbox was to be limited to just one tool, I would choose the tool of asking questions. But how do you do that?

In our Western culture answering questions is much more valued than asking questions and that is why we tend to tell. In order to involve others, build relationships, and solve problems asking questions and listening are much more important tools. At a conference on listening in healthcare it was stated that 80 percent of diagnoses concerning patients can be made while only listening. However, to achieve this it is also essential that we learn to ask the right questions.

When you ask open questions—such as who, what, where, when, why, how, and how often (also known as 5xW, 2xH) —you will get an image of the way of thinking of the other person. By asking these questions—in the workplace, based on our own observations—you and the other can learn together. And the answers can also be immediately tested in reality.

Asking questions starts with your own attitude: one of modesty (with regard to your own knowledge) and sincere interest in the other person and his answers. A Lean leader is most effective when he positions himself as a student, when he is curious, and asks open-ended questions.

After you have defined the problem by observing and asking questions it is time to investigate the cause of the problem. Asking questions is also very valuable here. As said before it is important to continue asking questions until you have found the root cause of the problem. By removing the root cause of the problem, you can prevent the problem from recurring.

For this purpose, a tool has been developed called "Five times why." This tool teaches you to ask "why" or "what is the reason?" a problem occurs and next ask why that is. The "five times" stands for the fact that you have to keep on asking sometimes five times (or more often) to get to the root cause of the problem. You have to keep in mind that people are rather sensitive to the "why" question. When asked this question people often feel like they are being accused of something. It is better to ask questions such as, "What is causing this?" or "What is the reason?"

Show Respect for People Who Do the Work

Lean strives for a culture of continuous improvement while being respectful to people. Most people do have some idea of what continuous improvement means. But what does being respectful to people mean?

In general people have their own interpretation of respect. For a Lean leader it goes further than respecting people as individuals, their origins, religions, and so on. First of all, it's about respect for humanity, respecting people for being human. In the Lean philosophy people are the most important and this means you will have to take into account everyone's possibilities and limitations.

With being respectful to people we mean in particular being respectful to patients and the people who do the value-adding work. Those who work directly with patients. You not only respect the work they are doing but also their opinions and ideas about the problems they encounter in their workplace and the possible solutions to these problems.

The best thing you can do as a leader is to let people grow, to help them improve themselves. Being respectful means that you also are challenging people, even outside their comfort zones. All this to encourage them to develop themselves. In doing so they first have to feel safe and secure. You create this safety by listening to people while not being judgmental.

And by looking for the problems and their causes in the system of work rather than in individuals. However, this is not easy and it requires a lot of your coaching skills. In Chapter 8 you can read about how to take the first steps in this.

Student's Thoughts

How are you going to apply the Lean principles and mindset in your own work as a leader?

1. How do you create and monitor the purpose of your team?
2. How do you engage people and make them your most important source of creativity and growth?
3. How do you create a culture of continuous improvement?
4. How do you make sure you focus on the workplace—where value is added—and that the processes really are getting better?

How do you develop the lean leadership skills in yourself?

1. How will you learn to observe? What are you going to observe and for how long? Why that? What are you going to do with the results?
2. What questions are you going to ask to whom? What answers and reactions do you expect?
3. How do you make people feel respected and safe? How do you deal with human errors? How are you going to develop people?

CHAPTER 4

Make Problems Visible at the Source

On a daily basis doctors and nurses are confronted with problems and mistakes. You can think of wrong medication, running out of supplies, forgetting something you have to go back to, or treatments that afterward turn out to not have been necessary. You can easily conclude through observations and conversations with patients and healthcare providers that the processes in healthcare are far from perfect.

Every process that is not perfect has to be managed. This means that management will always be needed because no process will always be perfect. This is different from what is sometimes claimed. There are many healthcare professionals who somehow suffer from management—or rather from their managers—and therefore think that management is a waste and should be eliminated. Why is this? What makes us think that management has no added value? Apparently, there is a gap between what we expect from management and what actually happens.

In order to better understand this gap, the first question we need to ask is, "What does management really mean?" In this book we define management as the processes by which you take care of your (care) process:

1. Let it do exactly what it needs to do (i.e., the care process meets all standards) with the desired outcome as a result: safe and with compassion, the right care at the right time in the right place at the right cost for every patient.
2. Always adapting to the changing needs of patients.
3. Constantly improving and innovating.
4. Continuously monitoring in such a way that any deviation from the desired condition is immediately visible at a glance and dealt with.

Together these four processes form your management system. Your management results, that is, the extent to which your four management processes meet the above ideal picture are strongly determined by how you manage. In this book we limit ourselves to two ways of managing: *traditional management* and *Lean management*. If you want to apply Lean management it is important that you also understand how and why others approach it differently.

Traditional Management

Traditional management is the most commonly used way of managing. It is very likely that you will also come into contact with this way of managing in your work. Traditional management is aimed at maintaining and controlling the status quo (the current condition).

Traditional management is characterized by the following:

- The managers—often from the second or even third level above the shop floor—are responsible for management and carry it out. The title of these people usually also is "manager."
- The manager focuses on the results, that is, the outcomes of processes. Often these are solely financial results such as the budget. He or she monitors the budget and if the actual expenses are out of line with the budget he or she intervenes.
- The manager has the task of decision maker. This means that the manager is expected to know how to solve problems and that only they can determine whether something is a good idea or not. Managers are the only ones who are allowed to spend money. This usually means that if your action to solve a problem is not on the budget there will be no money for it.
- Support departments are at the service of the managers. Whether they can help solve a problem is up to the managers. This is often accompanied by long action lists and many meetings with fellow managers to coordinate and set priorities.

- The manager is only interested in *big* problems. Problems that directly affect the results. He is not interested in the daily *small* problems such as lack of materials or equipment failures. Employees have to solve them themselves. Managers don't have time for that.
- People are the cause of problems because they do make mistakes. The question of guilt—Who is to blame? Who is responsible?—is central to solving them.
- The manager wants a hassle-free environment. The aim of a traditional management system is therefore to ensure that there are as few problems as possible. If there are problems, you want them to disappear as quickly as possible.
- The aim is to organize people, for example with hierarchy, organograms and job descriptions, so that it is clear who is responsible for what, who may decide what and who must (or may not) do what.

As you will probably understand in a traditional management system it is very unattractive for employees to report problems. That's why this hardly ever happens. Often under the guise of "Nothing will be done about it anyway."

Lean Management

We offer Lean management as an alternative to traditional management. In our experience Lean management fits better with people who want to improve their performance and that of their team continuously.

You can't improve if you don't know what your problems are. That's why Taiichi Ohno said, "Not having problems is the biggest problem you can have!" The goal of Lean management is to make problems and deviations from standard visible so that you can learn and improve.

Lean management clearly has different characteristics than traditional management such as:

- Management takes place as close as possible to the primary process. Preferably the people who do the work—such as doctors and nurses—manage the process themselves. Team leaders and managers help healthcare professionals by providing direction, by coaching, and by ensuring that standardization, training, process improvement, and innovation take place.

- Management is focused on the process and making adjustments if the process does not do what you expect it to do. Process management means for example that if you discover that a certain medicine has run out you ensure that it is ordered before you start your next activity.
- The healthcare professionals are the decision makers. They determine what is right for their patients and how problems can best be solved at that moment so that processes can continue.
- Team leaders, managers, and support departments are at the service of the workplace and the people doing the work. As a leader you make sure that in case of a problem you:
    ○ Immediately make the right help available.
    ○ Bring the process back to the standard.
    ○ Limit the resultant damage.
    ○ Determine the root cause.
    ○ Let everyone involved learn from it.
    ○ Prevent it from happening again.
- Problems are seen as development opportunities and as opportunities to learn and improve.
- Expectations and objectives are clear to everyone. Every employee in the organization—from doctor to board of directors, from bookkeeper to nurse—knows his or her contribution to the goals of his or her team and the organization as a whole.
- The intention is to organize the work (not the people): who does, what, when to serve the clients (patients).

As a first step in developing a Lean management system an improvement board is being put up on each group in a residential counseling center for mentally disabled people. Every practical problem that employees and clients run into they write on the board after which they discuss, analyze, and solve the problems together. Using this system, they were able to implement on average two improvements per week per group.

If they would not have used this system their problems would not have been solved. They would have been left to other departments, discussed at the team meeting once every six weeks or solved temporarily so that they would occur again or the solution would take a long time to implement. Now they improve and solve problems in a standardized way and train the new ways of working to each other. An additional effect is that employees feel much more involved. The team leader now has more time for structural issues. Team meetings run smoother and are more substantive because the small, daily problems are no longer on the agenda.

Blame the System

A fundamental difference between Lean management and traditional management is the way you deal with problems. How you think about problems, how you solve them, and where you look for the causes have a big influence on the extent to which you actually improve the work.

Research into nurses' problem-solving strategies (Tucker and Edmondson 2002) showed that nurses are currently solving problems without any help. This makes them feel good about themselves because working in this way they are doing over and over again what is necessary for a patient at that moment.

However, if you independently and directly correct your mistakes and solve your problems—without further communication and analysis—you make it virtually impossible to tackle the real causes.

A consequence of this way of solving problems is that it is much more difficult to learn from them together. Furthermore, people who are in the best position to solve the problem are structurally not involved. In fact, they are not aware of the existence of the problem. In the long run this can cause overburdening and even burnout because it only solves problems temporarily. So, your problems will keep coming back. We know this way of solving problems as *firefighting* and the solutions are mostly *workarounds*.

The disadvantages of this way of solving problems are reinforced by the fact that in traditional forms of management the question of blame stands central. You look for the person who caused the problem and blame him or her. The focus here is on the person who made the mistake, usually a healthcare provider. The more serious the consequences of the mistake the angrier we become at that person up to and including disciplinary matters.

A recent study by research institute Nivel in the Netherlands shows that doctors feel criminalized, attacked, and angry during a disciplinary case (Laarman, Bouwman, de Veer, and Friele 2019). This has negative consequences for their health and functioning.

We want disciplinary cases to lead to prevention of mistakes in the future. Do we overshoot our goal by putting the blame question first?

We can only prevent mistakes when we learn from them. That seems to be hindered here because:

- Sharing information is no longer in everyone's interest.
- If guilt is proven or negated the analysis is finished.
- The focus is on the major incidents.
- People are less open to feedback.
- The vast majority of the causes——that is, those in the system—are often left out of consideration.[1]

But what else can you do? What can you do as a leader or manager to ensure that you solve problems of doctors and nurses on a daily basis, learn from them and prevent them from coming back? You already have so much to do!

---

[1] W. Edwards Deming stated, "In 94 percent of situations the cause of a problem is in the system of work. Only in 6 percent of the cases are problems caused by individual employees."

First of all, you can offer support by regularly observing and talking about the problems people experience in their daily work. With the knowledge you gain in this way you can involve the right parties such as support departments. You can then work with them to ensure that the doctor or nurse can get on with the patient as quickly as possible by containing the problem. This will be experienced as support because the healthcare professional can then continue to take care of the patient instead of having to search for supplies or information and leaving the patient.

If you are on the floor with all those involved at the place where the problem actually occurs it gives you the opportunity to investigate the cause and learn from the problem. This will help you to ensure that the problem will not recur. You have to create a safe environment for this so that people are willing to share their problems and will not have the feeling that you are questioning their competencies or that you are trying to blame them. Never blame the people but blame the system and the process in which people work. Usually the root cause of problems and mistakes lies there.

Finally ask the healthcare professional for ideas for improvement and implement them so that you confirm that you have really listened to them. In this way you use their knowledge, experience, and creativity and you will create support. This will speed up the implementation of the necessary countermeasures.

Make your support, communication, and implementation of improvements a structural part of your daily work as a leader. Value your team for their willingness to share problems and for their improvement ideas.

In 2004 Mrs. Mary McClinton died at the Virginia Mason Medical Center (VMMC) due to a medical error: She was injected with chlorhexidine instead of a contrast fluid. Both fluids are transparent and were in similar stainless-steel scales.

VMMC's response was typical of what you expect of a Lean management system:

1. They gave complete openness about the error also to the media.
2. They were looking to blame the healthcare system—a management responsibility—and not the individual healthcare professionals.
3. They installed a patient safety alert system to detect and deal with all abnormalities and (near) incidents in advance.
4. Every year they still honor Mrs. Mary McClinton.

This has had an enormous impact on their safety culture and the number of incidents: it has been greatly reduced (Kenney 2011).

Manage the Process

Unlike traditional forms of management, Lean management focuses on managing the process in order to achieve the desired results instead of just managing the results. Lean management assumes that right, stable processes give right, stable results. Managing the process means that you monitor whether the process deviates from the standard. If so, you see that as a problem and—if necessary—you stop the process (!) and take immediate measures to bring the process back to standard.

The fuel level light in your car indicates that your tank is almost empty. Of course, you will refuel before you come to a standstill. You design your system of mobility based on the desired result (e.g., getting to your destination on time). You monitor the process of driving along the way and adjust in case of deviations. In this example your system consists of an authorized driver, a car, highways, and a filling station every 60 km. You then use process indicators (e.g., fuel light) to determine whether or not you need to adjust (whether or not to refuel) to ensure you reach your desired result (destination) (Orelio 2021, Chapter 8).

This example implies that in order to be able to manage your process you will have to make all deviations and problems visible at the moment they occur.

Problems Are Opportunities for Development

Making problems visible instead of making them disappear offers not only the possibility to solve them directly at the source but it also offers the opportunity to learn. Every problem is therefore an opportunity for development. Think of it as one of your primary tasks as a leader to develop your team and its individual members. By making problems immediately visible and tangible you create creative tension. This challenges people to come to a solution.

When discussing, analyzing, and solving problems together you learn more and more about your work processes. You also will develop your creativity and problem-solving skills. The more experience you gain in improving the bigger the problems you can solve independently.

By discussing problems directly—the moment they occur, when they are still small—you can easily and safely experiment with different countermeasures. This will teach you what works and what doesn't. This also contributes to everyone's development.

Visual Management

An effective method to manage your process is by using visual management. First of all, visual management means that you visualize your targets, plans, and standards. Then—in the same graph, table, or place in the process—you make the actual performance visible so you can compare them. The goal of visual management is to make problems visible by making sure that everyone involved can see at a glance whether there are deviations from the desired state. These deviations or problems are then investigated and dealt with. You will learn from this as a team and spread the acquired knowledge throughout the organization. In this process the leader has the role of coach (Orelio 2021, Chapter 4).

Three Enemies of Ideal Healthcare[2]

In Lean management we talk a lot about problems and about making them visible. But when do you actually have a problem? Here we speak

---

[2] Orelio 2021, Chapter 2.

of a problem when your actual condition does not correspond with your desired condition, your standard, or ideal. As long as your processes are not perfect you have problems and you can continue to improve. In order to help you identify problems at the earliest possible stage the three types of problems you may encounter in a care process are discussed below. These three are your "enemies" because they stand in the way of ideal care for your patients. We present them in the order in which you can best tackle them because one problem reinforces the next.

Overburden

First of all, there is the problem of *overburden* (excessiveness, impossibility, or unreasonableness). This occurs when you try to use your capacity 100 percent or more. Or if you say "yes" to questions or assignments that you can't really handle. This causes your process to come to a halt when there is a small variation in demand (e.g., workload) because there is no room (e.g., resources) to absorb this small amount of extra work. Waiting time theory teaches us that with an occupancy rate (the part of the time a person or device is scheduled) of more than 80 percent lead times increase exponentially and the matter of overload arises. This leads to extreme waiting times for patients, stress among employees, and "bullwhip" effects (i.e., increasing variability, see the second type of problem) in subsequent processes and sometimes even in the entire chain or system.

In the long term overload will cause your devices to be depreciated more quickly and people will become burned-out because they have to perform continuously at the peak of their abilities while making no noticeable progress. So, you should tackle overburden first. It may be necessary to—temporarily—"add water,"[3] that is, additional resources because for example you are working with too few people or too little inventory.

Unevenness

The second type of problem is *unevenness* (variability, nonuniformity, and irregularity). Unevenness means that a varying amount of resources

---

[3] See Chapter 2.

are needed, that the process is or has to be executed differently, or that your process has variable outcomes. Maybe you make poor use of your resources because sometimes there is a lot of (or too much) and other times there is very little work for the available capacity of people, rooms, or devices. Variability is tiring and can lead to errors and waste of capacity—the third type of problem.

Waste

The third type of problem is *waste*. Meaning, capacity is lost in dealing with problems. In care processes we distinguish three types of activities: value-added activities, nonvalue-added but necessary activities and waste. Waste is any activity or step in a process that from the patient's perspective does not add value. An exception to this is for example a legal obligation such as sending an invoice. These kinds of activities—which do not add value but are necessary—cannot be eliminated but must be carried out as efficiently as possible. In summary waste is:

- Everything that does not add value.
- Everything that does not help the (internal customer or) patient.
- Everything the patient would not like to pay for.
- The above provided there is no legal requirement.

In order to learn to see and recognize waste a list of the so-called seven deadly wastes has been made by Taiichi Ohno (Ohno 1988) supplemented later with the "waste of people's potential." Together we call them the "7+1 wastes." For healthcare these 7+1 wastes are (Orelio 2021, Chapter 7):

1. Defects
   - Incidents such as postoperative infections
   - Medication errors
   - Wrong diagnoses
   - Unnecessary pain or suffering
   - Miscommunication
   - Incomplete files

2. Overproduction
- Care for which there is no need
- Non-indicated care
- Preparing medication, in advance
- All sorts of "batching"

3. Inventory

Accumulation of:
- Work
- Materials
- Medicines
- Data or documents

4. Transport
- Patient transport
- Supply

5. Movement
- Searching
- Walking
- Turning, reaching, bending
- File routes

6. Over-processing
- Overdiagnosis
- Double registrations
- Too much information
- Meetings where no decisions are made or actions are taken
- Signatures
- Checks
- Correcting errors

7. Waiting
- for access to appropriate care
- for equipment
- for information

+1. Unused talent
- Working below your skill level
- Working above your skill level
- Don't let people think for themselves
- Don't ask for and implement people's ideas

Exercise

Look for examples of the "7+1 wastes" in your own workplace and share your examples with your team and other colleagues.

Self-Management

There is a great deal of interest in self-management in healthcare. Organizations such as *Buurtzorg* (the name of a home care organization in the Netherlands) have shown that you can successfully provide care while not having managers when you let employees in teams take care of their own affairs. It is deliberately stated while not having *managers* because it does not mean that you can do without *management*. You still want everyone to do the right things for patients, with or without managers, in a financially healthy way. What is needed for this?

If you want healthcare professionals to manage a process themselves it requires a matching management system. This management system must ensure that employees at the workplace:

- Know at the first possible moment that there is a problem or abnormality.
- Do not forward the problem to their colleagues and patients.
- Have the authority to stop the process.
- Have the skills to analyze and solve the problem.
- Have the necessary help immediately available.
- Can resume their work as quickly as possible.
- All learn from it.

Daily Improvement, Respecting People

Only through intensive collaboration between all disciplines in the care process can patients receive the right care at the right time. In order for your team to "work" in the right direction you need to have a clear understanding of the purpose of the process and the collaboration. In other words, you want to have a clear idea of the collective added value for

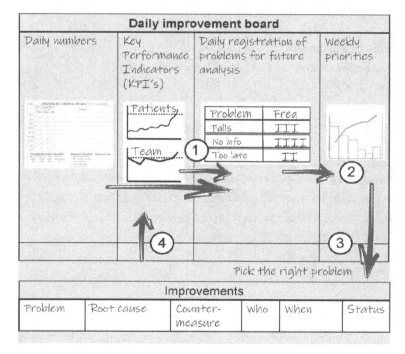

Figure 4.1 Visual management board for daily improvement

your patients. You make this added value visible so that you can see at a glance whether the right things are happening and whether there are any deviations (see Figure 4.1 for an example of a visual management board for daily improvement).

Discuss how your team has performed on a daily basis so that you can hand out compliments and make adjustments if things have gone wrong and then learn from them. Adjustments are always made in the direction of True North: Added value for patients with minimum efforts and costs. Test and improve standards on a daily basis and discuss performance with the entire team.

When you are looking into how things are going every day—or even more so with every patient—it will also prevent you from losing (read: forgetting) the facts about your performance and problems. When working this way people also will account for their own performance and contribution to the team in a safe, process-oriented manner on a daily basis. A well-known example of such a daily accountability is a huddle or a stand-up meeting. A huddle is a short, stand-up meeting usually at a board on which the performance, actions, and agreements are made visible. The team discusses performance and problems with the aim of involving everybody and which starts them thinking about and coming up with improvement actions.

One of the tasks of your system is to detect, analyze, solve, and prevent any deviation from the standards, targets, and the future state of the process. To this end you should install a so-called andon[4] (a possibility to immediately call for help) in the workplace. For example, a traffic light so that your colleagues and your supervisor know that something is not right and it's also urgent so that they can come to help as quickly as necessary. Offer the opportunity to discuss the performance of the day with each other. Problems that the team cannot solve is escalated to the next managerial level. And if necessary, all the way up to the executives.

Leader Standard Work (LSW)

A system only works when you actually stick to the agreed ways of working with all those involved. Especially as a leader you have to work in a disciplined way so that you show and emphasize the importance of your management system. To this end develop your own standard work. The standard way of working of a leader is called Leader Standard Work (LSW).

LSW provides a clear fixed rhythm for noticing, discussing, and addressing deviations from the process standards. If you implement LSW correctly your team members know where they stand because it answers questions such as "What is important," "When do I see my supervisor," and "How do I get involved." Disciplined adherence to your LSW provides predictability and peace of mind, which prevents you from the feeling of and the need for "troubleshooting." An additional reason for LSW

---

[4] Andon is a system developed at Toyota which is intended to give employees the opportunity to call for help in case of a quality or process problem by means of a visual signal. Everyone at Toyota is authorized (actually obliged) to use the andon and thus stop the production line!

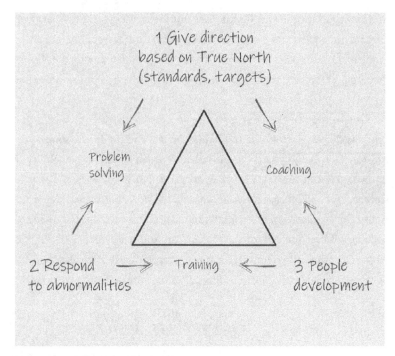

Figure 4.2 The Lean leadership triangle

is that it leads to exemplary behavior: not only healthcare professionals but also their leaders are having, following, and improving standards.

In order to standardize you need to know your processes. As a Lean leader you have three major work processes that are linked to your responsibilities (see Figure 4.2 for the Lean leadership triangle).

Your first responsibility is to give direction by formulating—together with all those involved—your ultimate goal—True North—and the challenges for the coming years.

Second, you will (help to) set standards for what needs to be done. Then you ensure that the people who do the work jointly create standards for how they can best do the work. These work standards should then be trained and followed in order to create a stable care process. The standards also serve to make deviations visible so that they can be responded to.

Third, you take care of process improvement. The developed care standards are your basis for this. As a leader you ensure that the right people are involved. You coach them to improve methodically and develop themselves.

How to Create Your Own Leader Standard Work

In order to create your own LSW, you can start the following step-by-step plan:

1. Design your ideal calendar (What do you ideally do, what process, when, where, for how long, how often, with which result?)
2. Analyze your current calendar (e.g., the current use of your time) and compare it with the ideal.
3. Formulate a target calendar (as a step toward the ideal) and determine when you want to achieve it. Create a "template" of your target calendar to compare with the actual calendar.
4. Regularly compare the actual use of your time with your target calendar and your plans for that day or week (Ask yourself: How long did the activity take? Was I there on time? And did I leave on time? Did I get the results that I expected from my activities? Did I do what I planned to do?).
5. Analyze the differences and find out the causes.
6. Develop countermeasures to eliminate the causes of reaching your target calendar.
7. Reflect on your progress and learnings.
8. If you systematically stick to your target calendar return to step 1.

To arrive at an ideal calendar, you need to know the calendar of your clients: When do they do what and where? Which are their routines and operating patterns? This is what you want to know so that you can attune your calendar to it. Keep in mind that as a Lean leader it is your team that is your most important client. Your boss isn't!

Student's Thoughts

1. How do you deal with problems?
2. What do you do to learn from problems and prevent them from coming back?

3. How do you support your team members with the problems they encounter in daily practice?

4. How are you going to make problems visible in the processes for which you are responsible?

5. What does your leader standard work look like? Is this ideal?

CHAPTER 5

Stabilize

The importance of stabilizing is nowhere more obvious than in healthcare where people's lives are at stake. In the event of a traffic accident, a heart attack, or a brain infarct the first objective is to stabilize the patient. When you ask, "How is the patient doing?" stability is almost always part of the doctor's answer. Only when the patient is stable you will look at how you can further improve the patient's condition.

If you want to improve your process it actually works exactly the same way. First you will have to make your process stable before you can improve it effectively. Otherwise—as with patients—you run the risk of unintended or unexpected effects that worsen rather than improve the situation. An unstable process is unpredictable and therefore unreliable. So you have to lay a foundation first by stabilizing it.

When your process is unstable and therefore always produces different, unpredictable results you don't know exactly where you stand now or whether the intended change is an improvement. At that moment instability is the first problem to address. Your first target condition is a stable process. Creating a stable process requires a plan in which you look for the root causes of instability.

Eliminate Overburden

Being busy is highly overvalued. When people are active, the machines are running, or when beds are moving through the hallways, we feel that the hospital is very productive. The other side of this is that if that doesn't happen—when people stand still or the hallways are empty—then we judge that as unproductive. As a result, we often are planning work for our resources, people, or equipment for 100 percent of their capacity because that's when we—so we believe—get the most done. In practice however this is not true.

If you work at 100 percent of your capacity, then you can

- not absorb any variation,
- not recover, and
- do no maintenance.

Variation is always there and it is everywhere: A patient is unexpectedly planned in between other appointments or an operation takes longer than expected. Just two examples and you probably have many more of your own. You can only absorb this variation if you have a buffer. Working at 100 percent capacity therefore leads in the short term to extreme waiting times and stress among employees.

In the long term it increases the risk of health problems in people—such as burn-out—but also accelerated wear and tear and depreciation of equipment. It also turns out that if you always have to perform at your peak you are more likely to make mistakes and keep repeating them because you don't notice them being so busy.

Prolonged poor performance (read: long waiting times and unreliable processes) ultimately results in patients running away toward another provider. As it were your patients solve the problem of overburden for you. Don't let it come to that!

Another word for overburden is "unreasonableness," which means that managers are behaving unreasonably when they overload their people with work. If you respect your people you would do everything to avoid overburdening them.

In order to prevent overburden, you will have to retain part of your capacity to deal with unexpected situations while not disrupting the entire planning. So, before you can stabilize your process you must first eliminate the overburden in your system. This requires strong leadership because it goes against traditional management thinking.

To do this use the three Lean leadership skills (Chapter 3). First, look for symptoms of overburden such as complaining patients or absent employees. Observe the situation like waiting lists, calendars, or planning and the actual way of working. Ask questions about this to investigate why people are so busy. Often this concerns their focus and how they set priorities. Ask questions about this.

An important question is, "How do you know if this work is needed now." People regularly are doing work that is not or not yet necessary. If you can eliminate this work or have it done when it is quieter you can easily free up capacity. This way you don't have to add capacity because it's too busy. By paying attention to overburdening you show respect for the people doing the work. Certainly—with overburdening—it is important that you let people know that it is not their problem and that you are prepared to take their capacity into account.

If the situation demands that you work hard make sure that this is ergonomically correct and that there is room to recover. One question you can ask here is, "How do you ensure that you can maintain this activity for years." This question also focuses on reducing overburden. Organizing the work in such a way that people can keep it up for years should be the goal of every manager. Once you have made sure that this is the case it is not a problem to work harder occasionally.

Monitor How Your Process Behaves[1]

Once you have tackled the overload of people, equipment, and consulting rooms you can start assessing whether your process is stable. In order to know whether your process is stable you will have to monitor your process to find out how the process behaves. You will look for the voice of the process—as it were—in order to hear how it is doing as you would with a patient.

For this you use a *process behavior chart* (see Figure 5.1 for an example). This is made by measuring the chosen variable—such as patient satisfaction in this case—and placing the measured values in a graph one after the other. Then you calculate the average and the upper and lower natural process boundaries. These natural process boundaries lie at +3 sigma[2] and –3 sigma of the average. Then you put the lines for the average

---

[1] A book that extensively explains how to measure, chart, and analyze the behavior of your process is *Measures of Success* by Mark Graban (2018). We keep the explanations and examples here simple. Processes can also behave in a more complex, yet stable way: for example, descending or ascending.

[2] *Sigma* stands for the standard deviation of your process and tells you how far away a part (a certain percentage) of your measured values are from the average. Calculating sigma is a standard feature in most spreadsheets.

and the process boundaries also in the graph. You expect 99.7 percent of all your data points to lie within the natural process boundaries of plus and minus three sigma.

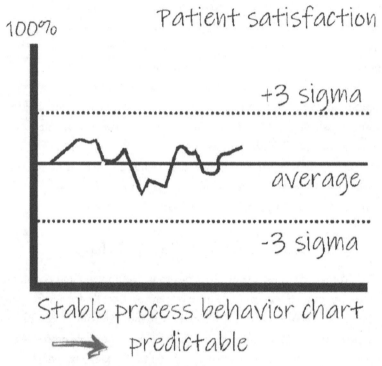

Figure 5.1 Process behavior chart (example, stable process)

Note: These are not target lines but only indications of how the measured variable of your process behaves. They are guidelines to determine whether your process is stable or not. So, you should not judge them. They only represent the current condition of the process.

The Rules for (In)Stability

Once your process behavior chart is ready you can use this graph to assess whether your process is stable for the variable in question. Your process is stable if it behaves predictably (like the process represented in the process behavior chart in Figure 5.1). The process moves continuously in a *normal* way around an average value and between the process boundaries. A stable process therefore also has variation but this variation is random, is within limits, and is predictable. We call this variation *common cause variation*.

In case of instability there is *special cause variation*. The causes of this variation are special because they are not an integral part of the process. They represent special circumstances that will have to be removed in order to stabilize the process.

To determine whether your process is stable there are three rules. If one or more of these rules apply to your chart then your process is unstable. In other words, your process is stable if none of these rules apply (see Figure 5.2 for a visualization of the three rules for instability, in a process behavior chart).

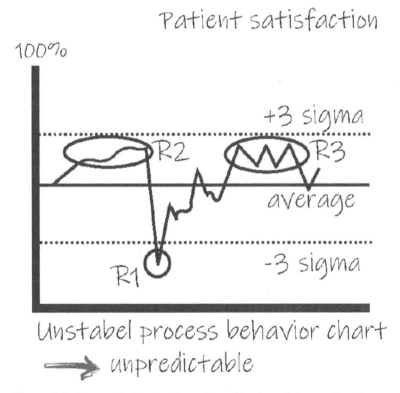

Figure 5.2 Process behavior chart (visualization of three rules of instability)

The three rules for instability are:

Rule 1: A single data point is outside the process boundaries.

Rule 2: Eight or more consecutive data points are on the same side of the average.

Rule 3: Three of the four consecutive data points are closer to the same process boundary than to the average.

Eliminate "Special Cause" Variation

Does your process behavior chart comply with one of the rules for instability? This means that your process is unstable and that you have special causes of variation. It is up to you to identify these special causes. Special causes are circumstances that normally do not occur in your process. This fact helps you to locate them. So, ask yourself, "What were the special circumstances at the time of the special cause variation"?

Then you can ask yourself why it is that the relevant data points in your process behavior chart comply with one or more of the rules. You can then ask yourself why that is the case. You continue asking until you have found the root cause(s) of the special variation. Do not make assumptions, but prove that you have found the right cause. Continue to eliminate special cause variation until your process is stable.

Reduce "Common Cause" Variation: Standardize

When your process is stable it means that all variation is normal, random, and therefore statistically predictable. You can now use the average and the process boundaries (based on the standard deviation) to predict which values to expect in the future. However, the value of an individual measurement is based fully on chance and thus a random number. So, there is no point in taking action on this individual value. This often goes wrong when managing processes. We call this "managing noise." Here noise is another word for "normal" or better known as "common cause" variation.

By managing noise, meaning overreacting, you cannot improve your process, but you can waste a lot of time and cause frustration. It can also cause a lot of stress the moment you hold people accountable for common cause variation. However, they cannot be blamed because it is a characteristic of the current process. If you don't like the performance of a stable process you will have to improve the process. This requires that you change the process itself and not the people who run it.

If you want to improve your process first reduce the variation and only then improve the average performance.

To reduce common cause variation, you will also have to understand what causes this variation. Unlike special cause variation common cause variation is not about incidental causes but about chronic causes of variation. They are—as it were—ingrained in the process.

Variation can be external. In that case the variation is caused by, for example, ever-changing numbers of patients per day or week in the emergency room. You have little influence on this and that is why it is called external. Limit the impact of external variation by preparing for it as much as possible and by adjusting your capacity where possible to the actual demand.

There is also internal variation. This means that the variation is the result of how you have set up and organized your process. For example, internal variation is caused by different people using different ways of working. Or that you are planning in such a way that you either run or stand still. Try to avoid internal variation. Standardizing your process and working methods is a very effective method to reduce or even eliminate internal variation.

"Yes, but ... Every Patient is Unique!"[3]

Standardization is one of the most controversial issues in healthcare when it comes to Lean thinking. Possibly this is because we still confuse standardization with uniformity and its excesses as in the days of Henry Ford (early 20th century) who said to his customers, "Everyone can choose their own color of car, as long as it is black." Think, for example, of the use of certain brands of devices or specific treatment methods where it is stated that "because this device or this treatment works with us you should all use this device or this treatment as well." This while each individual patient and each situation is different and therefore probably requires a different approach.

---

[3] Orelio 2021, Chapter 13.

How you treat a specific patient at a particular moment is determined by that particular patient and his specific condition. And the healthcare professional has to adjust to this by continually asking the question, "What can I encounter in this patient at this stage of the treatment process?" A checklist—a well-known form of standardization—can help here. However, keep in mind that it is not about the checklist but about the process of ensuring in advance that you have taken the right measures and precautions.

This is similar to the situation when you go sailing. Then you don't know exactly what kind of weather it will be. So, you set yourself up and you make sure you have everything on board: different sails, a rain suit, compass, radio, and so on. You don't standardize the adjustment of your sails or the clothing you put on but it's your preparation that you standardize. In other words, you try to standardize the process so that you know what to do and have the right tools available for each situation you might encounter.

Also, in the care process there are many similarities between different patients and how you help them (each patient makes an appointment, comes for a consultation, has blood tests, etc.). Surely you don't rethink these processes over and over again? It is best to take these steps in the best way you know at this moment so you don't waste time reinventing the wheel. Standards for the routine processes save time and space in your head, which makes room to pay attention to the patient and his specific condition.

When you see standardization as an aid to make the process reliable and next improve it, then it becomes apparent that the care process is becoming more flexible. Good standards stimulate people's creativity and make room for it. They help you to get most of the uncertainties out of your work in such a way that you get predictable outcomes. This prevents you from being distracted by "troubleshooting."

A standard is designed in the right way when it helps you to make deviations visible at a single glance at the moment of performance. A standard is a tool to know whether you are applying the best possible working method but above all to make problems and opportunities for improvement visible. In fact, standardization is the foundation of and a prerequisite for continuous improvement. When there are no standards no improvement is possible because in that case you cannot answer the question "is it better?"

Now do you have to standardize everything? No, because when you would do this you are running the risk of making standardization the objective—which it is not. Standardization is just a means to an end. It is a way of knowing whether you are doing the right things safely at the right time, in the right quantity, in the right way. It is the way to build quality into your process.

Levels of Standardization

But how do you standardize? A great deal of standardization takes place in the healthcare sector usually in the form of protocols, policies, and quality systems. Why should you pay attention to it anyway if it already is happening? It requires extra attention because the standardization methods—that is, the way in which we design the standards in healthcare—often turn out to be ineffective. What's more the right people are not always involved in developing, setting, training, and following up standards.

From my many visits to hospitals and conversations with healthcare professionals I have learned that in practice people regularly do not follow the established standards or they follow them incorrectly so that the standards only represent a paper reality. How is this in your team or department?

So, it is important to apply an effective method when you want to standardize. But before you can answer the question, "How do you standardize effectively?" you need to define what standardization is.

Here we define standardization as the process for making, following, realizing, monitoring, and adjusting joint agreements about the desired performance, process, and way of working. Standards are the outcome of this process and can take many different forms. They can also differ greatly in content and for example the level of detail. Standards vary from the time of a meeting, a method of preparing medication, to achieving a certain result such as delivering a clean patient room.

Basic rules for the ideal standard are as follows[4]:

1. All work shall be highly specified as to content, sequence, timing, and outcome.
2. Every customer–supplier connection must be direct and there must be an unambiguous yes-or-no way to send requests and receive responses.
3. The pathway for every product and service must be simple and direct.
4. Any improvement must be made in accordance with the scientific method under the guidance of a teacher at the lowest possible level in the organization.

An effective standard is an agreement—a mutually agreed way of working—which everyone involved keeps up to. Another aspect of an effective standard is that you immediately notice if you do not follow the standard or do not achieve the specified result, so you can adjust your way of working or the standard before major problems occur. Effective standards make training, maintenance, troubleshooting, and improvement easy.

Now that we have determined what an effective standard is you may ask yourself, "How do we usually standardize?" and "Are our current ways of standardizing sufficiently effective?"

You may not always realize it, but verbal communication is the most widely used way of standardization. Maybe you recognize phrases like, "I told you so!" or "This is the 10th time I've let you know!" You feel the frustration in the words and the fact that the appointment, rule, or agreement has to be repeated over and over again. From this you can conclude that verbal communication is not really such an effective method for standardization.

Text is slightly less bad but also very often used and often the assumed right method for standardization. For example, we make appointments via e-mail, and communicate policy through extensive documents and protocols in which we describe in detail how we want things to go. Many pages of text that should make it clear how the work needs to be done. The problem with this is that we cannot remember all that is described and that there is a lot of room for interpretation in written documents.

---

[4] These rules are known as the *four rules-in-use* (Spear, Bowen, and Kent 1999).

This is because most texts focus on content and completeness instead of the best way to make sure people understand and reproduce it on the job.

Fortunately, there are more effective methods for standardization than these two. You probably even know them already, but you don't apply them sufficiently in your own work yet. What are these more effective methods for standardization?

You might want to think about traffic. When you are commuting for instance, you come across many examples of effective standardization. In order to increase effectiveness, you see the following standardization methods in traffic:

1. Visual[5] aids.
2. Visual controls.
3. Fail-safes or error proofing.

(See Figure 5.3 for examples of such methods of standardization at railroad crossings.)

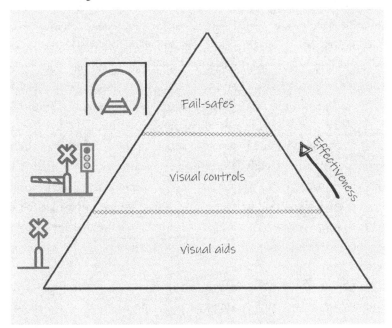

Figure 5.3 Standardization pyramid

[5] Instead of visual aids, you can also think about aids based on other senses such as hearing, smelling, sensation, or taste.

Visual aids indicate at the place where you need the information what the standard is or which rule applies. Road signs are an example of this such as signs carrying speed limits or priority rules. Visual aids help the driver to know which rules apply at that time for that part of the journey. This asks of the driver to remember the standard for that part of the road. He must decide for himself what this means for his driving behavior. This can certainly still go wrong. For example, because someone has forgotten the rule, missed it, or in some cases because he deliberately does not abide by it. Visual aids are indeed only tools and they still require alertness of the user. Visual aids can also be found in hospitals such as signage or warning stickers for areas where hazardous substances are used.

Visual controls are more effective. Visual controls such as stop or warning lights indicate which behavior you need to show at that moment. In traffic they tell the driver whether to continue or to stop. So, the driver only has to be alerted the moment he approaches an intersection. The visual controls are giving him clear signals as to what he is expected to do. This can also go wrong, but the chance of this is much smaller than when just a visual aid is used. Visual controls ask less of someone's memory. You also don't have to make a conscious choice to change your behavior unless you are still inexperienced. Experienced drivers automatically slow down when they see a red traffic light. In a hospital you will find visual controls mainly at Intensive Care (IC) where patients are continuously monitored. If a problem occurs a light comes on or an alarm sounds.

If you want to be sure that people adhere to the standard at all times you make fail-safes. Here you design the standard in such a way that it can't go wrong. In traffic you can think of overhead crossings. For example, you drive over a viaduct over a railway track so it is impossible to hit the train with your car. An example of fail-safes in a hospital are the connections of different gases. You can't connect these to each other's pipeline because then they won't fit.

From the above examples you can deduce that effective standards require a lot of work and consideration. The more effective the methods for standardization are the more expensive they are to produce in most cases. However, effective standards take way less time, energy, and alertness to adhere to. Effective standards are usually more efficient. On top of that you are able to avoid a lot of mistakes and eliminate the need for corrective work. Especially when it involves people's lives, prevention is preferable to cure. Besides correcting mistakes often involves high costs.

Many forms of standardization can be found in the hospital either effective or less effective. In my experience there is still a lot of room to standardize work processes more effectively. What is the situation in your hospital?

SDCA

As can be seen from our earlier definition we look at standardization as a process. This process consists of four steps. We present the standardization process and the four steps as SDCA: Standardize, Do, Check, Act. You can see this as the counterpart of PDCA (the learning cycle). They are like yin and yang complementing each other. Or as Taiichi Ohno put it, "Without standardization there is no improvement" (Ohno 1988).

We have provided each of these steps with support questions in order to determine whether you have taken a step in the right way.

1. S—Standardize: Do you know the standard?
2. D—Do: Do you follow the standard?
3. C—Check: Did you get the desired outcome by following the standard? If not, why?
4. A—Act: What did you learn? How can you improve (yourself)?

Ultimately the leader is responsible for the standardization process. You can best manage standards by applying the principles of Lean leadership. By observing yourself at the workplace and asking questions such as:

1. S—What is the standard here? How should the work be done?
   (a) Content?
   (b) Sequence?
   (c) Timing?
   (d) Outcome?
2. D—Is the standard followed? How do I know that the work is being done correctly?

3. C—Are there any deviations from the standard? How do I know that the outcome is error-free and that it is right the first time? How do I know that this is the right care for this patient?

4. A—How do I act as a leader in case of deviations?

(a) Bring the situation back to standard.

(b) Agree on how to improve:

    i.   Do nothing.

    ii. Teach the standard.

    iii. Improve the standard.

Job Instruction (JI)

Standardization is an intensive process and requires a different mindset of people especially when they are trained with the idea of professional autonomy. This often means that they mainly develop and apply their own methods. Apart from the fact that this leads to variation in working methods between different healthcare professionals, it also results in a limited flow of knowledge about working methods and their specific dexterity between experienced and less experienced employees.

To address this problem, Job Instruction (JI) has been developed. It's a part of TWI. TWI stands for "Training Within Industries" and is a highly standardized approach with the initial goal to increase the productivity of the U.S. weapons industry during World War II. This was a difficult task because it was mainly inexperienced women who worked in the workplace as the men were often sent to the front as soldiers. In addition to the industry, TWI was also used in other sectors such as hospitals where very positive results were achieved (Graupp and Purrier 2012).

TWI is aimed at supporting first-line managers such as supervisors. TWI is the foundation of continuous improvement while being respectful to people. Standardization, improving processes, and developing people are directly interwoven in TWI.

One of the elements of TWI is Job Instruction (JI). JI is a very effective way to standardize and train people. JI is intended to enable people to carry out the necessary tasks in the right way and to become proficient in these tasks.

JI does not make protocols and other standards superfluous. It only provides a method to instruct people in an effective way. Using JI (team) leaders learn in their role as Job Instructor to analyze, standardize, and train tasks in a way that ensures that everyone including inexperienced employees can perform the tasks safely, flawlessly, and efficiently.

Manage the Four M's

In Chapter 4 you learned that the first management responsibility is to ensure that you let your (care) process do exactly what it is supposed to do (i.e., the care process complies with all standards) and is always resulting in the desired outcome.

First of all, this requires a stable process that you have to keep stable. You keep your process stable by focusing on the standards and by ensuring in advance that your process can and will perform to standard. You need to manage the inputs.

A simple process to manage inputs for yourself and your team is a morning huddle[6] in which you discuss the input standards, the so-called *Four M's*: Man (People), Methods (protocols), Materials, and Machines (Devices). You prepare each day by asking yourself for each M, "What do we need? Do we have everything in the right quality and quantity? If not, how do we solve this so that the patients receive the right care at the right time"? You do this not only for the care processes but also for supporting processes such as administration or training.

Support your management of the four M's with visualization. For example, create a huddle board on which the team—for man, methods, materials, and machines—can see at a glance what the plan is and what is actually happening. This will make deviations visible and will ensure that you know what you still need to arrange in order for the day to go according to plan. A nice side effect is that this allows the team to manage their own inputs and processes which means that not all responsibility is transferred to the leadership.

---

[6] A morning huddle is a short, daily stand-up meeting, in which a team prepares for the day. Sometimes the morning huddle also includes an evaluation of the previous day and the discussion of KPIs and improvement proposals.

Student's Thoughts

1. Where on your team or in your department do you suspect overload? How do you deal with it?
2. What is the behavior of the processes you work in or are responsible for? Are they stable?
3. What important standards are there for your team and the care for your patients? How do you make sure you keep your agreements and meet the standards?
4. What do you do in case of deviations to the standards or unmet patient needs?

CHAPTER 6

Improve Your Process

Although the following quote has also been attributed to many others (often wrongly), I would like to believe that it comes from the motion picture *28 Days* with Sandra Bullock in which she is addicted to alcohol and ends up in a rehab clinic. One of her therapists says, "Insanity is doing the same thing over and over expecting a different outcome." What does this statement teach us about process improvement? In short it indicates that if you want different (read: better) results, you will have to change (read: improve) your approach, your process. So, process improvement is about influencing your results by adjusting your process in the right way.

You begin your improvement process with the question, "What problem am I trying to solve?" A problem is just nothing more than the "gap" between your current situation and your desired situation. We distinguish four levels of problems (Smalley 2018). Each of these levels has a specific approach to solving them:

- Level 1: *Troubleshooting.* A reactive process in which you correct deviations and abnormalities as quickly as possible and bring the situation back to the (mostly assumed) standards as you understand them at that moment. This is usually just symptom management and often will lead to fake solutions (solutions that do not address the real cause of the problem). In practice we often call this *firefighting.*
- Level 2: Remedy a deviation from the standard. A structured problem-solving process aimed at identifying and, if possible, eliminating the root causes of the problem. The steps you take at this level are: define the problem, set targets, analyze, implement countermeasures, do tests, and standardize.
- Level 3: Working toward a target condition. This requires a process in which you continuously improve in order to

further increase your performance. Your goal is to achieve new, better standards, or conditions beyond your current performance.

- Level 4: Innovation. An unlimited pursuit of a vision or an ideal condition while using creativity and synthesis. This leads to radical improvements and unexpected processes, products, systems, or value for customers beyond what is currently available in the market. To give direction you define your challenges and strategic goals based on your vision or True North.

These levels help you to choose the right problem to address, based on the need for improvement, the quality of your current processes, and the problem-solving capabilities of your team and yourself.

It is important to realize that there are no shortcuts to results. So, you can't just change something and then think it's going to be okay—no matter how genius your idea is. In order to be able to improve your process you have to understand it first. You will have to realize that in order to achieve better results 80 percent of your efforts will go into researching the current condition. You need to investigate and understand where you stand and why you are not getting the desired results. This enables you to break up your problem in smaller and more concrete pieces and get closer to the source of the problem.

What Is a Process?

To get better results you need a better process. But first we have to define what a process is. A process is a set of interconnected activities in a certain order. These activities transform inputs into outputs. You deliver these outputs to customers in order to solve their problems or fulfill their needs. If you succeed to meet the needs of your customers—your patients—you deliver added value (see Figure 6.1 for a basic model of a process).

For example, think of a care process in which a patient with a broken leg enters the hospital (input) and then leaves the hospital after diagnosis and treatment (process) with his leg in plaster (output). After six weeks the leg has healed, the plaster cast is removed, and the patient can exercise pain-free again (added value).

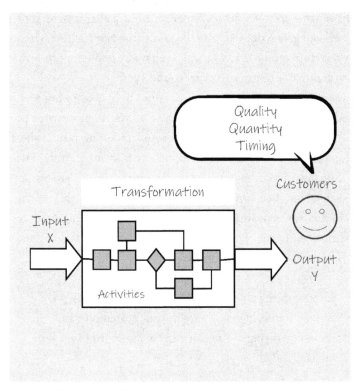

Figure 6.1 Process model

The Definition of Improvement

Now that we have defined what a process is and we know that you need to improve your process in order to improve your results, you can ask yourself how you know if something makes your process better. In other words, how do you know that you are solving the right problem? After all you don't want to blindly solve all the problems you may encounter. It is very important that you solve the right problem. Therefore, before you start improving your process you should answer the question what you need to improve instead of starting with the question what you can improve. This question results in a long list of all kind of problems: big and small, important and unimportant. The question "What do you need to improve?" provides you the focus. It focuses your energy and that of your team on the important things. Namely the problems that stand in the way of you and your team achieving your goal (i.e., better results).

To support this, we define *improvement* as a step toward your goal whereby your goal is derived from the ideal: True North. Process improvement therefore means that you realize a target condition, improve your results, and that it brings you closer to the ideal.

However, process improvement does not only need to improve your results. It certainly is just as important that you improve your process in the right way. Here the right way means respecting people and their development. If carried out in the right way (according to the values of Lean), process improvement is in fact a great way to develop people's leadership skills, their problem-solving capabilities, and their craftsmanship. In this way you work on all the elements that are important for job satisfaction. As Daniel Pink points out in his research and the resulting book *Drive* job satisfaction requires

- purpose (being able to contribute to a higher goal),
- mastery (achieving excellence in your profession), and
- autonomy (being self-reliant and having control over your work).

All this increases people's motivation and involvement (Pink 2009).

"Batching": The Source of All Evil

According to our definition a process is a pattern of work: what do you do in which order. One of people's most persistent work patterns is batch work or *batching*. Batching means that you first finish or help the whole stack or group (batch) after which the whole stack or group goes to the next step in the process where you work on them or help them as a stack or group. Batching comes from mass production. It is based on the idea that you are most efficient when you do as much as possible of the same type of work as quickly as possible. This results in collecting (batching) the same type of work and avoiding changeovers as much as possible. You usually check afterward—when you have finished your work (the whole group or stack) —and then you correct any errors that occur.

You can find a recognizable and visible example of batching at an airport. First of all, we are all queuing up to check-in. Next we all queue up in front of customs to undergo the well-known security check. Finally, we all queue up again to board the plane. And then our flight hasn't even started yet. The plane itself is also a form of batching, which means that hundreds of people fly together once a day to a fixed destination by no means always their final destination.

The example of the airport shows that batching leads to long queues and slow processes. Sometimes it takes up to two hours to get from your car to the plane while hoping that it will leave immediately. In healthcare there are also many processes in which people are batching, just think of the waiting lists, rows, and rooms. But why are we doing this? We organize our processes like this because we—and especially managers—collectively assume that this is more efficient.

If you place a queue in front of the check-in and the airline employee can always perform the same task directly after each other than that seems and feels more efficient. You are constantly at work and—on the face of it—very productive. After all, working this way you produce a whole pile of checked-in passengers. But this is really a misconception, a fallacy at the heart of the difference between traditional and Lean management thinking. Where does this misconception come from? Why is it that batching is not as efficient as it seems?

The first reason is that "batchers" measure their success by their individual or departmental performance. As a result, they do not see the results of the entire process and system they are part of. In addition, they believe that the results in the rest of the process is not their responsibility. This leads to suboptimization. In other words, the assumed high productivity of your department does not lead to high productivity of the entire process. This is because you all are creating extra actions for yourself and others.

The second reason is that batching can and will result in all kinds of different forms of waste.[1] However, the problems caused during batch processing and the enormous waste it generates are usually not visible or noticeable. In the example of the airport for example some of the problems and waste are visible and perceptible but unfortunately especially

---

[1] See Chapter 4 for the "7+1 wastes."

for the passengers. They have to stand in line for a long time and walk long distances. It is difficult to get help and when mistakes are made this often concerns the whole group because you only find out later what is wrong. Here batching also seems more efficient, but it is not the supplier or the worker who absorbs the problems and experiences the waste but the customers are.

The third and most persistent reason is that we grew up with a batch mindset and that we do not experience the disadvantages of batches as problems. In fact, the accounting methods and performance indicators we use are confirming the success of batching. This supports our beliefs (see reasons one and two) and thus batching remains our preferred working pattern. After all it is for good reason that a Lean transformation is difficult to execute. It requires that we let go of a hundred-year-old way of collective management thinking.

But if batching is not the right way because its results are lower performances, it leaves the customer with waste and it hides your problems then how can you get rid of it? The answer is by transforming your processes and systems to *one-piece flow*.

The Ideal Process: "One-Piece-Flow"

In short Lean management strives for maximum added value at minimum efforts through continuous improvement and respect for people. What does this ideally mean for your team, your processes, and your patients[2]? In other words, what is the vision or True North for a Lean process?

First, Lean means the output of your process is exactly what your patients need to solve their specific problem and it perfectly meets their needs. Patients receive the right care in the right amount at the right time and in the right place; safely and with compassion and no waste or struggle.

Second, the input of your process contains exactly the right people, materials, methods, and machines (the four M's see also Chapter 5)

---

[2] Where it says "patient(s)" you can also read "(internal) client(s)". After all, not everyone works directly with patients.

allowing you to produce the right outcome (output) in one go with minimal effort.

Third, your processes follow the principles of one-piece flow (or in healthcare one-patient flow). This means that all process steps add value and are carried out in one go at the desired speed, patient by patient, and no unnecessary waiting time. The result will be top quality, an extremely short lead time, and the lowest costs per patient and for the system.

Although these performances are fantastic this is only part of the importance of one-piece flow. The real secret lies in the fact that this way you cannot hide your problems (in stocks, overcapacity, or queues). If a problem occurs your process will stop almost immediately giving you a chance to learn about your process and where you can do even better. This stimulates continuous improvement and provides daily challenges to the team and therefore the opportunity to develop themselves. One-piece flow is therefore, besides the best possible process, an element in your Lean management system with the purpose of making problems visible. But is one-piece flow really ideal? Is it really more productive than batching? Find out for yourself by watching the video and do the exercise *Fold envelopes* (Pereira 2014).

Requirements for One-Piece Flow

Before you turn everything around and start working in one-piece flow you have to realize that this is a vision—True North—for your process. It is something to strive for by eliminating all the problems and waste that stand in the way of the flow of your process. Then when you no longer seem to have any problems you let your process flow faster and remove more waste in order to make more (smaller) problems visible and thus further improve.

In the metaphor of the boat (see Chapter 2) you lower the water level and let the water flow faster meanwhile making the debris (read: problems) visible on the surface. In practice this means that you reduce your inventory, buffers, and capacity, make less space available, and deploy fewer personnel so that you will get into trouble sooner.

You will understand that this places quite a number of demands on your care system. The conditions to enable and maintain one-piece-flow are as follows:

1. *A stable and very reliable process.* You have to avoid that your process will be constantly at a standstill because of the many problems you have. This will create chaos and therefore there will be no flow. Aim for more than 80 percent reliability. This means that in more than 80 percent of the time the process does the right thing at the right time. (Read in Chapter 5 how to create a stable and reliable process.)

2. *Built-in quality.* This means that you can tell that you are doing the right things during the execution of the process and not only afterward. The person who carries out the process is responsible for this. The agreement is "error free from me"[3] or in other words you do not pass on errors to the next process step. The healthcare professionals must know at the moment of action whether the right thing is being done. Subsequent checks are out of the question in the case of flow because they then find out far too late whether there is a problem. For the leader of the process this means that he or she has to ensure that people have the knowledge and tools to assess the quality of their work on the spot.

3. *Stopping the process.* If you cannot guarantee the quality of your work you need to (automatically) stop or slow down the process. It is essential that the authority or perhaps the duty to do so lies with the people who carry out the work.[4] In a Lean process you never pass on a defect to the next step in the process and certainly not to your customers.

4. *Immediate help* in case of a problem is needed because otherwise the whole process or even the whole system will come to a halt. There are no buffers in one-piece flow so you need to ask for help immediately to solve the problem, to let the process flow again, and then to iden-

---

[3] This statement comes from Scania in Zwolle, The Netherlands, and can be found in the model of their management system (Luttik 2011).

[4] Gary Convis, former Toyota President, said: "Employees only have to do two things: show up at work and pull the cord" (Liker and Convis 2012). At every workstation on the assembly line at Toyota there is a rope (Andon cord) that employees pull when problems occur so that the line slows down or comes to a standstill.

tify the cause of the problem in order to learn from it and to prevent this problem from recurring in the future.

5. *Working at the pace of the customer.* You only do something when the next step in the process is ready and your patients need the activity. Take care to have all the successive process steps in the chain connected to each other with a simple and direct signal. In Lean terms this is called *pull planning*: your client pulls your process as it were and thus sets the pace. The opposite method is called *push planning*: you push as it were your patients, materials, or work through the process. It is the planning and available capacity of the care providers or suppliers that determine the pace and not the patients.

6. *Keep your batch (or series size) as small as possible*—preferably one. This requires that you keep short your changeover times (well under 10 minutes).

7. *Don't allow waste* such as piles of inventory and waiting times into your process because apart from costs and frustrations this will hide your problems. When there is waste in your system you don't know if you are doing the right thing at the right time. This requires a continuous effort from management. Don't allow waste to creep back into your system!

How to Approach Process Improvement?[5]

It is advisable to start small with yourself and your own processes. Here small means a small problem or improving a single activity that you can influence yourself.

Small is not about ambition. With every improvement try to have a big impact on the problem you are tackling. Some good rules of thumb for your minimal ambitions are to double or to halve your current performance. For example, to double productivity or to halve the amount of errors. Then when you are more experienced you tackle bigger and bigger problems and involve more and more people and different departments.

---

[5] Orelio 2021, Chapter 7.

As a result, your learning process will run in parallel with your improvement process.

During the improvement process you focus on taking many small steps that together lead to the realization of ambitious goals. Make sure that in the beginning you set a goal that leads to a relevant and noticeable change.

Ideally your improvement strategy should include the following substantive steps:

1. Establish your ideal—your True North: your ideal process and your ideal outcome.
2. Define your problem or challenge(s).
3. Start with improving what bothers you (your team) the most. To do this you analyze the current condition.
4. Set challenging and concrete time-bound improvement objectives.
5. Eliminate overload and special causes of variation.
6. Stabilize your processes and make them reliable for example by creating standards. Standards form the basis for further improvement.
7. Create flow in your process.
8. Align your process with the current customer demand (read: patients' needs).
9. Maintain the flow and keep improving in the direction of True North.

Now which problem are you going to start with?

Imaging Is 80 Percent of the Work[6]

For many the standard response to a problem is trying to solve it. This means that you take measures to solve the problem while not really knowing the problem and its underlying causes. This often leads to symptom management, workarounds, and "fake solutions" (solutions that do not solve the real problem). Your problem-solving or improvement process is most similar to what we have called "troubleshooting" in this chapter.

---

[6] Orelio 2021, Chapter 9.

It is much more effective to start a process of imaging first to create a shared vision of the ideal and your challenges or problems. For an effective improvement process it is important to spend a relatively large amount of time—about 80 percent—to define and research your problems and challenges, the current condition, and the target condition. This is essential to prevent you from jumping straight to the solutions and doing the wrong things. Only after you have done your due diligence you can draw conclusions and take the right actions!

A shared image of a problem is also important for the commitment and support to solve the problem. Therefore, you should involve as many people as possible who are part of or connected to the process that has to be improved. Do not come up with solutions and only after that start to involve the people. When involving people think of patients, different disciplines and departments, suppliers, and support staff. In other words, everyone you need for a successful change in your process.

Examine the Current Condition[7]

After selecting and scoping the improvement you want to achieve or the problem you want to solve, you map out exactly what the current condition is. You do this to find out exactly where you stand in relation to your final goal. In doing so you try to answer the question, "What is the current condition in which the problem is occurring?" The more concrete and detailed you answer this question the more you learn about the problem and the circumstances in which the problem occurs. This provides insight into possible causes.

Go to the place where the problem manifests itself. Observe the current work process in order to get a deep understanding of how it works. Collect the facts—if necessary supplemented with measurements and conversations with the people who carry out and experience the work such as healthcare professionals and patients. For example, follow the route a patient takes or observe a nurse during the application of an infusion. Then start asking questions about this whereby it is not the person but the process that is the subject of discussion.

---

[7] Orelio 2021, Chapter 9.

Questions that support understanding of the current condition and help define the problem more clearly are the following:

- Who has the problem?
- Why is it a problem?
- Where does the problem occur?
- What exactly is happening? What is the process in which the problem occurs?
- When does the problem occur?
- How often does the problem occur?
- How much impact does the problem have?

By mapping the current condition, you can often divide the problem into subproblems, which you next analyze and solve piece by piece. This helps to create focus and work on concrete issues. The more concrete your problem is the easier it is to identify the causes and come up with the right countermeasures.

Set Your (First) Target Condition[8]

Do you have sufficiently mapped out the current condition? Do you have correctly defined the problem together with all those involved on the basis of the facts? If so the next step is to set the target condition. The target condition is an image of the current condition but then formulated positively (improved) and in the future (in 2–6 weeks, for example).

The criteria for a good target condition are as follows:

- It is—visible, noticeable, and measurable—a step in the direction of the ideal—True North.
- It answers your challenge.
- It describes both the desired process and the desired outcome(s).
- It is a condition of which you do not yet know the solutions.

---

[8] Orelio 2021, Chapter 9.

Take Many Small Steps (e.g., Improve Continuously)[9]

As soon as you have your target condition clear the planning process is over and the actual improvement process can start. Improvement is most effective when you solve your problems at the source meanwhile eliminating the root causes. At this stage you start looking for the obstacles that stand in the way of achieving your target condition. Next you investigate and tackle them by experimenting.

Identify the obstacles (causes) by asking the question, "What prevents us from reaching the target condition?" By asking this question you focus your attention on the relevant obstacles. You then clean up these obstacles one by one. Why one by one? Why don't we make a plan to clear the obstacles all at once?

You do this because you learn something from every step you take which in turn determines your next step to take. Each step also changes the condition you find yourself in and thus your perspective on the obstacles that exist. In addition, this step-by-step approach ensures that you will find out more quickly when you are moving away from your goal. It makes it easier to adjust so there is more chance that you follow the most efficient route to your goal.

Finally, another important advantage of step-by-step improvement is that you learn the relationship between your actions and the effects they are having. With each improvement step you follow the PDCA cycle or Plan-Do-Check-Act.

A very effective tool for step-by-step improvement and learning is the *PDCA diary* (Mike Rother 2010; Download 6.1) in which you keep track of the steps you take to remove each obstacle and of what you are learning along the way. The PDCA diary is structured around the following four questions:

1. Which step are you going to take and when?
2. What effect do you expect this to have?
3. What actually happened?
4. What did you learn?

---

[9] Orelio 2021, Chapter 9.

(Download the *PDCA diary*, via the provided QR-code.)

Student's Thoughts

1. What is your preferred strategy for problem solving and / or improvement?
2. In what proportion do you spend time on research, analysis, and developing countermeasures when solving a problem?
3. What would make your current improvement process more effective?
4. Where in your area of responsibility do you batch?
5. Where do you have flow?
6. What could you do to create more flow?
7. Where will you start your improvement process?

CHAPTER 7

Develop Your Leadership

The starting point of a Lean thinker is that your results are an outcome of the process you use. So, if you want better results you will have to improve the process. But then who is going to do that? Ideally this will be the people who carry out the process. They are in the best position to understand and improve the process. However, they are not going to do this on their own. In any case this requires a vision, support, knowledge and skills, resources, and an action plan. In other words, this requires leadership from you! After all, someone has to take the first step and make sure that all the necessary elements are in place. Waiting for others to do something is ineffective and will make you as a leader redundant.

Improving results requires a process in several stages. It starts with developing yourself and your own leadership through which you learn to set the right example. You have to make sure that people can and want to follow you. Next you coach and develop others in your (improvement) team so that they are better able to solve daily problems themselves. Finally, you link the daily improvement process to the objectives and strategy of your organization so that you improve in the right direction.

I do not want to suggest a step-by-step plan when carrying this out. The above is a phased and cyclical process by means of which you become better and better in developing yourself and others and improving processes, getting results in the right way. This allows you to cope with ever larger changes. As you go through this process you always test your improvement process and leadership against the ideal of the Lean leader, starting with the four Lean principles and the three Lean leadership skills from Chapter 3.

An important question here is, "Are you willing to develop yourself, at the service of others?" Yes? That's good because that's the basic requirement for a Lean leader.

Principles of Personal Leadership and Success

In leadership development many think of courses, management development programs, and especially of gaining many years of experience in which you become wise through trial and error. This line of thinking is understandable because this is the most commonly used approach. But this method of leadership development has some disadvantages, one of the most important being that you yourself have virtually no influence on what you learn when and where it will lead to.

Leadership courses and management development programs are usually set up by others sometimes even from outside your organization. They provide you with ideal-typical leadership styles and skills. It makes you aware of the possibilities, but it does not actually change your own leadership. You will then have to work with your new insights yourself usually without supervision.

These insights are in many cases not in line with the expectations, preferences, and practiced leadership styles of others in your organization. However, these have much more influence on your behavior and thinking—and therefore on your leadership—than what you have learned in your courses and trainings. This means that your leadership mainly develops in a way that fits the culture of your organization.

The question we are trying to answer here is, "How could you get a better grip on your own development so that you can (also) achieve your personal goals?"

Takashi Harada has done extensive research into this. He asked himself the question, "How do I become successful in life?" To this end he mainly studied top athletes and developed his own method based on the principles he discovered. According to Harada (Harada and Bodek 2012), the most important four principles that will develop your leadership and will lead you to personal success are the following:

1. *Set a personal goal.* This is much more powerful than an imposed goal. A goal that comes from your heart motivates much more than a rational goal. When you have a personal goal, you take control of your life and your development. This is in itself a leadership quality.

2. *Be self-reliant.* Self-reliant means that you live in the knowledge that everything you need to be successful lies within yourself. So, you learn to trust yourself.

3. *Work with a coach.* The coach acts as a mirror, which is making (self-) reflection easier. The coach holds you accountable for achieving your goal and the plans you make to realize your goal. He dares you to disappoint yourself. After all being humans, we always come up with a story why things didn't work out. Disappointing another person—your coach—is much harder. A coach will strengthen your sense of responsibility.

4. *Serve others unconditionally.* The most important characteristic of a Lean leader is modesty. You don't want your ego to get in your way. You train your modesty by showing others that you don't feel too good to do whatever comes up to do. Serving others also teaches you discipline and determination. It confirms that you are apparently willing to do anything to achieve your personal goals. In addition, whether you are a good leader or not is mainly determined by the quality of your relationships with others. The more you focus on helping others the more valuable people will find you and the happier you will be.

Analyze Your Self-Reliance

Before you immediately formulate a goal and go into the action, you take a moment and wonder how self-reliant you are. This largely determines your chances of success.

In order to examine someone's self-reliance Harada drew up a *list of 33 qualities of self-reliance* (Download 7.1, p78), including words such as courageous, competent, caring, self-assured, creative, and determined. This list you can use to analyze your self-reliance:

1. Give yourself a score of 1 to 10 for each of these 33 qualities.
2. Think of possible measures for those qualities you would like to develop further.
3. Put these measures in your plan.

4. See these measures through.

5. Work and reflect on your self-reliance daily.

(Download the *list of 33 qualities of self-reliance*, via the provided QR-code.)

Serve Others

Contrary to what you are probably used to, your plan does not start with your goal but with what you are going to do for others on a daily basis. Think of a daily service for the people in your personal life—your family, relatives, or people in your community. Then think of a daily service for the people in your working life—your patients, your colleagues, or your team.

It is best to start with these daily services to others before you start working on your own goals. Preferably choose something that causes you discomfort for example because you feel "it is beneath you" or something that you feel is not your job or responsibility. It is even better if others didn't expect you to be willing to perform the activity in question.

If you can't think of anything yourself ask the people around you. Ask them what they would like and what would really help them.

What Is Your Personal Goal?

It is very powerful when you have a personal goal (in life), but when people are asked "What is your purpose in life?" they often stay silent. Sometimes they even feel embarrassed when they don't know what to say. In many cases they have never been asked that question before!

Maybe you will recognize the following. When I was young people around me used to ask me what I wanted to become later in life. The question was often asked out of politeness rather than out of real interest. They expected my answer to be focused on the goals of the school of society or the expectations of my parents. A missed opportunity as far as I was concerned.

So, here is the question, "What is your purpose in life?" Please take your time to answer this question. The question is more about how you want to live than about a specific result you want to achieve. To discover your purpose in life you can ask yourself the following supporting questions (Garcia 2017) in the order indicated:

1. What are you very good at?
2. What do you like to do? What is your passion?
3. What do others need? What can you do to help (many) people?
4. What can you do to make money?

For many of us the last question is often the first question we are asked or ask ourselves. This leads us to the idea that making money is the most important goal, meanwhile, disregarding ourselves, our qualities, what we love to do, and what others value us the most for. This can be very demotivating and can make people unhappy at work, so for example they want to retire as soon as possible.

So please start to (re)formulate your goal in life and take yourself as a starting point. Ideally the goal you have formulated is the answer to all four questions. You could call this True North of your life.

Once you have determined your direction in life it will be easier to formulate your personal goal for a certain period to come. You do this by comparing your current personal condition with your life's purpose and then ask yourself what would be a good step in the coming period (3–6 months) toward your purpose.

Your personal goal tells you something about when and how your process—your way of working—has improved and what improved results you expect this to bring you. Don't worry about the feasibility of your goals. It is especially important that your goal is concrete, recognizable, and inspiring. It may be something you actually think is impossible. Something that challenges you to rise above yourself.

Examples of personal goals are as follows:

- "On December 31, 2017 I published a book and sold 250 copies."
- "On March 1, 2015 I adapted our planning system so that the waiting list is cut in half."
- "On October 15, 2016 I developed myself in such a way that my team gives a score of 7.5 out of 10 for my leadership."

So where will you be in 3–6 months?

Why Is This Important for You?

It's important to realize that your goal is not a final goal. Goals are just a tool to improve, to become successful, and above all to be able to determine what is the right thing to do in this very moment. You determine the quality of your goal and therefore the chance to actually reach it by examining the underlying motives or in other words your motivations. To discover your motives you ask yourself, "Why is this goal important for me?" "Why do I want this?" To this end ask yourself, "What does this goal bring me and others in a material and immaterial sense."[1]

Experience teaches us that goals work best when they yield mostly immaterial benefits to others. It is interesting that these kinds of goals make us personally most happy. In other words when you focus on helping others you work on your personal happiness.

Find a Coach

One of the principles of Lean thinking is that you improve (yourself) continuously. This will only be successful when you continue to develop yourself and others. You cannot do this without help from other people. So, find a coach to help you to set and realize your goals.

Your coach is there to challenge you through seemingly impossible goals. While you are still unsure yourself, he shows confidence in you. He

---

[1] Material means tangible such as money or new products; immaterial means intangible such as feelings like pride.

makes it possible for you to learn and experiment safely, and he challenges you to leave your comfort zone. The right coach mainly asks questions and will give a few answers. At most he makes suggestions to meet a certain challenge. Above all he will let you wrestle with the change yourself and will encourage you to think in a different way. And last but not least, he is an example of the new way of leadership. The example you want to follow as an (upcoming) leader. Look for a coach who at least:

1. puts your goals and learning process first;
2. is honest with you so that you don't miss opportunities to grow and progress;
3. uses a proven successful method to achieve your goals; and
4. is frequently available, especially in the beginning so that you learn your new routines in the right way.

Develop a Balanced Plan

Now that you have a personal and motivating goal the question is how you achieve that goal. This requires a balanced plan that takes into account more than just the actions that are directly related to your goal. Balanced means that you include in your plan all aspects of your life that are important to you so that achieving your goal is not at the expense of other aspects of your life. It turns out that you have the greatest chance of success if you work on all these aspects during your improvement process or at least take them into account.

Harada uses four aspects of life in which you will have to develop yourself in order to achieve your goal and make your dreams come true. These aspects are

- mindset,
- skills,
- health, and
- daily life.

These four aspects give direction to the structure of your plan and help you to think broadly and balance your activities across all aspects of your life.

You analyze yourself and your life for each of these aspects and use this as input for your plan. You ask yourself questions such as:

- What are my strengths?
- Where do I need to improve?
- What are my successes and what are my failures?
- Which obstacles do I expect to face in the future?
- Which habits are going to help and which ones are hindering me?

You use your answers to know what to work on and what to maintain. You add to this the measures you have devised to increase your self-reliance.

You put all your insights and ideas about what you need to do to achieve your goal in an overview—a mind map (see Table 7.1 for a part of the mind map I made for my plan to publish my first book). You make such a mind map—of your plan to reach your goal—in three steps:

1. Put your personal goal for the coming period in the middle.
2. Put around it all the aspects of life you need to work on in order to reach your goal.
3. Put around each aspect the activities needed to improve the aspect in question.

After creating a mind map you make it executable. You need to know what to do, when, or how often. To create a concrete plan, you first distinguish between tasks (individual activities) and routines (habits which you can train yourself until they become automatic). For clarity mark them with a T and an R in your mind map. Next you set a date for your tasks and you create an order of priority for your routines because clearly you can't do everything at once. However, you can make sure that you plan in such a way that you work on your goal every day and consistently. Do the easy things with the greatest impact first. To do this you regularly ask yourself the focusing question as formulated by Gary Keller in his book *The One Thing* (Keller and Papasan 2014), "What is that one thing I *can* do, such that by doing it everything else will be easier or unnecessary."

Table 7.1 Example of a balanced plan for reaching a personal goal.

1	2	3	1	2	3	1	2	3
[1] Harada LT-form (APR) (T)	[2] Read professional literature, every day (R)	[3] Online Sales Course (APR) (T)	[1] Meditate everyday 5 min (R)	[2] 90 percent score on routine checklist (JAN) (T)	[3] Harada diary, every workday (R)	[1] Upside-down website (SEPT 18) (T)	[2] 10K subs—module 3 (AUG) (T)	[3] 10K subs—module 4 (SEP-DEC) (T)
[8] Santorini Seminar Lean Leadership - LLI (AUG) (T)	Personal development: - Harada - Lean leadership - Online business	[4] Harada training (APR) (T)	[8] Hackathon (FEB) (T)	Mental: - Positive - Future oriented - Flexible; stress-free	[4] Sports 3× per week (R)	[8] Publish blog—1 per month (R)	Build online business	[4] Give-away (JUN) (T)
[7] Read Mindset by C. Dweck (JUL) (T)	[6] Healthcare Event (MRT) (T)	[5] Certification Harada (DEC) (T)	[7] Plan for the week, time blocking: tasks, client and rest (T)	[6] Harada plan + planning (MEI) (T)	[5] Walk the dog, every day (R)	[7] Connect website to ESP (MAI) (T)	[6] Sell "Passport to the Gemba" (online) (SEP) (T)	[5] Offer online coaching on website (NOV) (T)
[1] Transcription (MAI) (T)	[2] Streamline Chapters (DEC) (T)	[3] Process feedback from editor (AUG) (T)	Personal development (B)	Mental (C)	Build online business (D)			
[1] Approach people on E-mail list (AUG-OCT) (T)	[2] Social media campaign (SEP-OCT) (T)	[3] Launch team (AUG) (T)		GOAL—31 December — Launch book and sell 250 copies				

Monitor Your Routines

Your new or improved routines are the real secret to success because they help you to actually change your behavior, your skills, and your mindset permanently.

Developing new routines requires discipline especially in the beginning. This is because you have to practice them consciously and this costs your brains extra energy, which it doesn't like. You will know this because you will feel uncomfortable and show other forms of resistance to practicing the new routine. You need discipline to get the extra energy and willpower you need to overcome this. When the new routines are becoming a habit, they will require less energy and discipline.

That is why it is important to start practicing a new routine on a small but frequent basis. Small because it will limit the energy you need and frequent because then something will become a habit. It is better to practice just one minute every day than 20 minutes once a week.

In order to stay disciplined and keep practicing and holding yourself accountable you should make your performance visible and report regularly to a coach. Therefore, you have to monitor the routines you want to develop. Make a list of your intended routines including daily services to your family or organization. Then fill in every day whether you have performed the routines in question. At the end of the month you evaluate this. Reliable tracking of routines is a strong indicator of your chances of success and achieving your goal. Successful people score at least 80 percent of the number of times they wanted to practice their routines.

Keep a Diary

Achieving your goals requires—in addition to a plan and its implementation—continuous reflection and adjustment. Especially if your goal is something you have never achieved before. The most important routine to be successful is the PDCA learning cycle.

Start recording for each day how you are going to work on your goals that day and which tasks you are going to perform. At the end of the day you evaluate this and reflect on the process, your behavior, and your experiences. Then you think about the adjustments you need to make to your plans in order to stay on track. By including this in a diary you force yourself to be consciously engaged in learning. By writing it all down you process everything better and you can consciously reflect on the results you are achieving. This is called *deliberate practice*. In addition—when you regularly pause and look back—you will notice and thus celebrate your successes. Otherwise you will miss them or forget about them. Just like all other newly learned habits keeping a diary takes time and energy in the beginning, but it will go faster and faster and eventually it will take about five minutes per day.

Personal Development through A3 Thinking

Yes, but . . . it is not all that easy to change. I'm very busy and I've been doing it in this way for years. No, it certainly is not always easy to learn new skills or change our behavior let alone our ways of thinking. If this applies to you too please use the Lean principles from this book to work on this. Then you will kill two birds with one stone: you will develop the desired behavior while practicing Lean thinking. This will gradually change your mindset as well. In this way it becomes easier and easier to make bigger and bigger changes.

Use the *A3 for personal development* (Download 7.2, p86). This is a Lean tool that helps you to

- structure how you work on your own development while spending a lot of time on investigating your behavior, self-analysis, and reflection;
- communicate your plans and progress with the people around you and with other people involved in your development process (in this way, they can follow what you are doing and why which will make it easier for them to help you and provide you with ideas and feedback during the process); and
- be coached easily because with an A3 you make your thinking explicit.

(Download the *A3 format for personal development*, via the provided QR-code.)

Student's Thoughts

1. What is your purpose in life?
2. What do you want to achieve the coming period in your (new) role as a leader?
3. What do you need to change?
4. What is your plan to realize your (personal) goal?
5. Who is your coach?

CHAPTER 8

Coach Others

What would your hospital or ward look like if everyone made it a little bit better every day by solving problems and learning from them? Would this be more effective than working on a project basis and taking big steps? Yes, it would! The pace of your improvement process would increase enormously and people would develop every day (see Figure 8.1 for the difference in improvement speed for projects done by experts versus daily improvement by everyone). Imagine that this would be the normal course of events, then a culture of continuous improvement and learning would emerge in which healthcare providers themselves would be in charge.

But how are you going to achieve this culture? How are you going to ensure that everyone—in your team—improves, learns, and takes charge of their own improvement process every day? The goal of a leader is to create more leaders and not just followers. The best thing you can do as a leader to accomplish this is letting people grow and make them better. To make sure that as many people as possible in your team participate in continuous improvement you need to train them. But who is going to do that? Ideally it will be you yourself being the leader of change.

This has two important effects. First, you transfer the change in this way in line with your own vision of the how and why. Second, you learn a lot yourself when you train others. So, if possible, you should play a role in the training of your team.

How do you do that? After all you are not trained as a teacher or a coach. First of all, you develop yourself and the basic skills needed for (leading) continuous improvement and learning. Next you are going to coach others.

There are two ways in which you have a major impact on people's development: unconsciously and consciously influencing them. Unconscious influencing is something you do every day through your behavior, your attitude, and the things you say or don't say. So, it is essential that

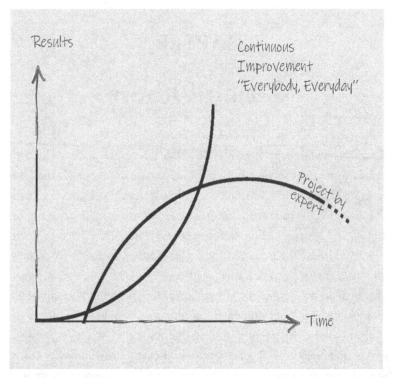

Figure 8.1 Continuous improvement versus projects by experts

you set the right example in how you behave on a daily basis. In addition, you can also influence consciously. You use a phased training process for this in which people practice deliberately, purposefully, and in a high frequency (daily) under your supervision.

Coaching for improvement also means that you challenge people—even outside their comfort zones—so that they develop and learn new things. However, they first need to feel safe and secure. This safety is created by listening to them while not being judgmental. Also, by looking for the problems and their causes in the system of work rather than in individuals. This is not easy and will require a lot of your coaching skills.

Phase 1: Create Awareness

When you want to train people, it starts—every learning cycle again and again—with awareness. By experiencing, seeing, and hearing people build up knowledge and learn for example what new methods look like and how they are built up. Their training in this first phase usually consists of courses, training sessions, company visits, reading, watching videos, listening to podcasts, and "last but not least" observing how others do it, like you for example (Orelio 2021, Chapter 11).

Be the Example

When trying to influence others as a leader it is important to realize that people don't do what you say but mainly what they see you doing. So, it is essential that you set the right example if you want to help people to behave in the right way. Former Toyota President in China Ritsuo Shingo called this "show them your back!" Meaning that you have to go first in the desired behavior so that the people who (want to) follow you can see what the intention is. If you behave in the right way then others are also inclined to behave in the right way. For example, he bought second-hand furniture for his office and drove a small company car to make people cost-conscious.

If you want the people you lead or work with to continuously improve (themselves) it requires that you exhibit the desired behavior and master the right skills that go with daily improvement and learning.

Where to Start?

What are effective skills and behaviors to create awareness among your team members and colleagues? What you can do right away is:

- be transparent about your expectations and goals;
- admit your mistakes;
- ask regularly what you can improve personally;
- experiment with new ways of working; and
- share your lessons learned and experiences.

A practical and effective way to work as a leader on a culture of continuous improvement and learning is to ask people every day, "What have you learned today?" Then let them share their answers for example through an app or in a short meeting and do the same for yourself.

Do self-reflection and set the right example this way. Mirror yourself every day to the ideal Lean leader. The ideal Lean leader observes, tries to understand situations, asks open questions, asks to find the root causes of problems, and shows respect for the people who do the work.

Phase 2: Improve and Learn Together

After the process of awareness, you let people apply the new method—under (your) guidance—until they have mastered the method. You pull up together with your pupil as it were. You let them prepare and apply (parts of) the method themselves in which you continuously coach them. Because of the intensity of this approach as a leader you are actually the only one who is able to be the coach especially because your behavior outside the improvement activities certainly has so much impact. So, you need to be aware of this. People sometimes react differently because you are "the boss."

"Just Do It": *Personal and Team Improvements*

Methodical improvement does not mean that you turn everything into a project. Above all methodical improvement means that you use the right method or technique for the problem at hand and stick to it. The size and complexity of a problem determine how much structure you need to bring the improvement process to a successful conclusion.

If you can solve the problem with a simple action, please do it. In this case we call the improvement method "just do it." If the problem is simple and can be solved by a single person but you don't know the exact cause you call it personal improvement. The method to apply is a one-page improvement proposal. In an improvement proposal you describe the problem, the root cause of the problem, and your proposal to remove this cause. In case of complex problems—with multiple unknown causes that require a diverse group of people and extensive research to analyze and solve the problem—you will work in a team-oriented way. You will form a multidisciplinary improvement team (also known as quality circles or small group activity (SGA)).

Multidisciplinary Improvement Teams

The objectives of multidisciplinary improvement teams are the following:

- To improve methodically
- To learn about your process and how to improve it
- To bring about sustainable improvement
- To develop people in their different roles.

Improvement teams are a great way to learn and improve together. It is a good way to structure your (project-based) improvement process and make it more effective when you want to solve larger or more complex problems.

The difference with traditional improvement projects is that in a multidisciplinary improvement team you put the development of the team members first. They are the experts, and they do the analyses and come up with solutions, in contrast to traditional projects where these roles are usually assigned to experts like staff advisers or even external consultants.

You organize such an improvement team around a mutual problem such as waiting times for patients or medication safety, which everyone is convinced is important to improve. This common interest helps to ensure that people are not distracted by personal or departmental interests and keep looking past them because of a higher purpose.

An improvement team ideally consists of five to seven people and the participants representing all the different disciplines involved in the problem or topic. Participation is voluntary but not without obligation. When selecting the team members make sure to look for people who have or want to develop leadership qualities and are able to include their colleagues in the team's improvement process.

The following roles are distinguished in a multidisciplinary improvement team:

- Team member: brings in knowledge, experience, and creativity; helps with the execution of the improvement work such as doing research and testing countermeasures.

- Team leader: stimulates and monitors the cooperation process between the team members; attunes with the client and structures the meetings.
- Client (often a manager or senior leader): challenges the team; mentors the team leader; helps to recruit the right team members; stimulates, and supports the learning process of the team members and the team leader; ensures that the objectives of the team are in line with those of the organization.
- Facilitator (e.g., a Lean coach): helps team members, team leader or client to be successful in their role; provides the necessary improvement and change management skills; monitors the methodical approach and ensures that the right tools are used in the right way.

In this phase of joint improvement and learning it is important that you as a leader have experienced each of the roles—several times—and thus grow toward the role you ultimately want or have to fulfill.

A3[1]

A tool that can be of great value to an improvement team—with the right guidance—is the *A3 for process improvement* (Downloads 8.1 and 8.2). The A3 is named after the paper size that people at Toyota used to record their plans, problem analyses, and improvements.

The A3 helps to:

- structure your improvement process;
- simplify communication within the team and with the various stakeholders;
- make the team's progress and thinking visible; and
- enable coaching.

---

[1] For learning how to work with and coach the A3, I advise you to read *Managing to Learn* by John Shook (2010). The book is special because it describes the perspectives of both the learner and the coach.

(Download the *A3 format for process improvement*, via the provided QR-code.)

(Download the *Applied A3 format "Door movements"*, via the provided QR-code.)

Phase 3: Coach from a Distance

In the third phase of the people development process it is time for the learner to continue independently. The training process is characterized by frequent (weekly or even daily) short moments of contact. You discuss assignments—sometimes one-on-one—mostly at the workplace. You help to make obstacles visible. You discuss them and allow people to make the lessons learned explicit.

The goal of you as a coach is that the learner in addition to mastering the improvement process learns to learn and think for himself about the problems he encounters. It is therefore important that as a trainer you avoid giving the answers.

The Coaching Routine[2]

If you want to train and coach people—to improve methodically—you will have to incorporate the methodology you want them to learn in your coaching.

Lean coaching therefore has a standard coaching routine—a set of questions in a certain order that will help you to learn how to coach improvement and to let people follow and learn a methodical improvement approach. This coaching routine—which you can also use as a support for your own learning process as a coach—consists of two stages (Rother 2010).

Stage 1 is the planning stage in which you develop a target condition for yourself and your team based on a challenge or problem facing the organization.

The steps and associated coaching questions in stage one are:

Step 1—Understand the direction

- What's True North?
- What is the challenge you face in the next one to three years?

Step 2—Examine the current condition

- What's the problem? Who faces this problem? Where, when, how, and how often does it occur?
- What is the current process? What is the current pattern? What is the current performance?

Step 3—Determine the (next) target condition.

- Where do you want to be in two weeks to three months' time?
- What does the target condition look like? What changes do you want to achieve in process and performance compared to the current condition?

---

[2] Orelio 2021, Chapter 6.

Stage two is that of continuous improvement and learning. In this stage you as a coach want people to learn step by step on a daily basis how to remove the obstacles that stand in the way of their target condition.

The coaching routine for this stage consists of the following steps with related questions (Rother 2010):

1. What is your target condition (on your way to your challenge—your ideal)?
2. Where are you now? What is the current condition?
3. Which obstacles are in the way of your target condition? Which obstacle are you working on now?
   (a) Which step did you take?
   (b) Which results did you expect?
   (c) What is the actual result?
   (d) What did you learn?
3. What is your next step? Which result do you expect?
4. When can we—coach and learner—reflect on this?

By applying the coaching routine consistently, a standardized and self-evident way to improve is being created. In this way it becomes a habit and part of the culture in which people continuously improve their own work and themselves through coaching by leaders and each other. Through the questions from the coaching routine you as a coach and the learner go through the PDCA learning cycle over and over again, obstacle by obstacle, thereby making it habitual and creating your new way of thinking. Tip: use aids such as the A3 and the PDCA diary during your coaching to structure the improvement and learning processes.

Feedback

Psychological research shows that people do 95 percent of everything they do unconsciously (Tiggelaar 2009).

So, it is very difficult to work on your own development and improve yourself only on the basis of self-reflection.

Fortunately, there is more and more attention for giving and asking for feedback. Feedback means that you give back what you have seen or how you have experienced something or someone. You give or receive feedback based on questions such as "What am I good at?" "What can be improved?" and "How did I make you feel?"

Feedback is important because it appears to be one of the most effective ways to achieve learning and improve your performance (Hattie and Clarke 2018).

Feedback is meant to compare what you actually do with the desired way to do it. This enables you to make adjustments when there is a gap. If you work without getting feedback, that is, without corrections it is almost certain that you are not doing things the right way. Feedback about customer focus, leadership, and others are standardized in many organizations in the form of among other things satisfaction surveys and performance reviews. A good development because it indicates that people want to learn and want to become better. The problem with these kind of measures for feedback is that there is usually a long time between your performance and the moment you get the feedback. This makes it very hard to truly learn from it and to work on the right issues.

Although it is effective, getting and giving feedback is difficult because it requires reflection. This means that you give back your observations while not being judgmental. The latter is difficult for many people. Judgments generally lead to emotions and feelings of, for example, guilt or shame. Or pride in the case of positive feedback. This seems okay but caresses or hurts your ego, which then gets in the way of further improvement or learning. Another unintended side effect of positive feedback is that others who hear this positive judgment sometimes project it onto themselves. They then get thoughts like "She gets this compliment and I don't so I am doing something wrong."

So, if you want to give feedback you will always have to be aware of the words you use, the situation you are in, the person you are giving it to, and the emotions and feelings it will evoke in different people. This requires practice and is best facilitated—in order to create psychological safety in the group—to be allowed to make mistakes and to get feedback on giving and receiving feedback.

Feedforward

In addition to feedback you can also work with feedforward. Feedforward means that instead of judging the past you give tips on what someone can do better in the future or should continue to do.

In short feedforward works as follows:

1. Choose to change one behavior to make a positive difference in your live.[3]
2. Describe this behavior to others.
3. Ask for two suggestions for achieving a positive change in the behavior.
4. Listen to suggestions and take notes without commenting on them.
5. Thank others for their suggestions.
6. Ask others what they would like to change.
7. Provide feedforward—two suggestions aimed at helping them change.

If you work with feedforward you agree that you don't talk about the past and just listen to the other person's ideas while not being judgmental. Just thank them for their input. If you follow these rules then feedforward is a psychologically safe, energetic, and effective method to work on behavioral change.

According to Marshall Goldsmith, the world's number one executive coach, "Giving and receiving feedforward only takes about two minutes. When asked to describe the experience with feedforward people use words like 'great, energizing, useful, helping, fun.' Whereas, [when asked about feedback,] few of us think of feedback as 'fun!'" (Goldsmith 2007).

---

[3] If you have trouble thinking about what behavior this should be ask the other person, "What can I do to be a better leader (employee, colleague, etc.)?"

Student's Thoughts

1. What culture prevails in your team, department, or organization when it comes to improvement and learning?
2. What roles do people have in the improvement process and how do they approach improvement?
3. What is your desired improvement process and what behavior do you expect from the people around you to make that process a success?
4. What development do people have to go through to achieve this desired state?
5. How are you going to help them?

CHAPTER 9

Align Your Improvement Efforts

When you have reached a system and culture of continuous improvement in your team it is a great result. People experience that you take problems seriously, your team grows, and you can help your patients better and better. However, this is no guarantee that you will contribute to the goals of your organization. It requires that you connect your goals with the organizational goals.

This asks for a collaborative process between the different layers in the organization. This collaboration is intended to translate end results—such as patient satisfaction, quality of care, or financial performance—into concrete actions. Actions that (teams of) care providers can take to improve and realize the organizational goals.

We call this cooperation process "catch ball" to indicate that it is not a one-way street but a dialogue in which you ask clarifying questions about the direction, the objectives, and the plans people have to achieve the objectives. You challenge each other and engage in research so that plans and objectives are based on the actual situation in the workplace. Plans and targets go back-and-forth between the different layers and parts of the organization, becoming clearer, more concrete, and creating commitment with the people responsible for realization of those plans and targets.

In order to determine during the process of catch ball whether your plans for improvement are aligned with the objectives of the organization, an important question is "What is your target condition?" When there is no target condition it is difficult to judge whether your changes are going in the right direction. Your next question could be, "How is your target condition linked to the long-term vision and challenges of the organization?" This is the litmus test for the success of implementing your improvement plans. Do you know how your actions contribute to the organization's strategy and goals?

> Suppose for example that a hospital wants to reduce the length of stay of patients. This could mean that the neurosurgery department is trying to shorten the recovery process of patients after hernia surgery. Subsequently one of the neurosurgeons—being the owner of this improvement—could conduct research into new operational techniques with the aim of achieving faster recovery while the quality stays the same (Orelio 2021, Chapter 12).

Put Your Patients First: Improve Your Value Stream

The most important thing in a hospital—the primary process—is patient care. Your patients are the reason for a hospital of being in business. They are who you should most consider when you want to improve. By defining your care system as the scope of your improvement process you optimize "automatically" in the service of your patients and prevent suboptimization, because the care system perspective helps you to judge the quality of your care and the added value of your processes from the patient's perspective.

When improving your care system, you focus on the chain of process steps that belong to a single patient group that share the same resources and process steps. In the medical world such a chain is often called a *clinical care pathway*. In Lean terms you call this chain a *value stream*. You take the value stream as the scope—the framework—of your system improvement.

It is important to realize that most hospitals have multiple value streams of varying size and complexity that are often intersecting (e.g., sharing resources). The organizational structure is often at odds with the value stream (see Figure 9.1 for a sketch of the organizational structure intersecting with the value streams). Value stream improvement therefore requires commitment from the entire senior management. How do you successfully tackle a value stream improvement?

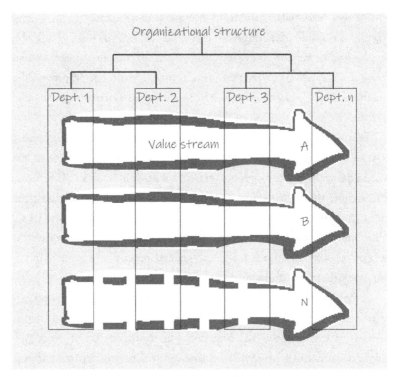

Figure 9.1 Value streams versus organizational structure

Value stream improvements are the responsibility of the management or executive team. They select the value stream you need to improve based on the following criteria:

1. Necessity to improve. Which value stream for example is unsafe, puts too much strain on the patient, has low patient satisfaction, or long waiting times?
2. Support from those responsible (e.g., senior management).
3. The amount of experience with value stream improvements. The more experience the more complex the changes you can handle (within your organization). If you have little experience then the ability to learn from the improvement process is an important criterion.
4. The chances of success (this is strongly linked to the first three criteria).

Involve (external[1]) help from the start—a facilitator (e.g., a Lean coach)—to guide the improvement and change process. Preferably involve him or her also in the selection process of the value stream you are going to improve. Be aware that it is almost impossible to improve value streams without a coach due to the complexity of system improvements and the challenges in thinking Lean principles demand.

To avoid making the improvement process unnecessarily complex it is wise in the beginning—when you have little Lean experience—to stay within the walls of your own organization with your analysis. This means for example that when improving the value stream of the surgical treatment of hernias you start your analysis when the patient reports to the clinic and that you end it when the patient is discharged. In that case you do not consider the processes of the general practitioner beforehand or the physiotherapist afterward.

After selecting the value stream the management team also takes care of the composition of the improvement team. Ideally you also involve patients in this process. The improvement team consists of many participants (sometimes up to 12) because many different departments and disciplines are involved. You do this on the basis of the following criteria:

1. Departments or disciplines involved
2. Informal leadership
3. Enthusiasm to participate
4. Personal development objectives of leaders.

Value Stream Mapping

An effective Lean tool for improving value streams is *value stream mapping* (Rother and Shook 1999).

A better name would be value stream analysis and design because that tells you more about the objectives of the tool. Value stream mapping helps you to map out the value stream in which process times and lead times are the most important performance indicators. Value stream

---

[1] Outsiders can more easily address sensitive issues because they have an independent position.

mapping makes it clear at a glance which parts of the process actually add value for your patients. The most important steps for making a value stream map and resulting improvement plan are as follows:

1. Determine the goal or added value of the value stream.
2. Determine the customer demand; how many patients do you need to help per period and calculate the takt time[2]; how much time is there between two patients?
3. Walk the value stream with your multidisciplinary team and literally step into the shoes of your patients. As you do this you note which steps you go through, measure the process times, register waiting moments, walking distances, and what problems there are for patients and care providers.
4. Display the current (actual) value stream on large sheets of paper: the process steps, the problems and data per process step, the waiting times, and (walking) distances between the process steps (see Figure 9.2 for an example of a simplified value stream map, current state).
5. Indicate whether the process steps are of value to the patient (or not).
6. Calculate the lead time(s): how long does it take for a patient from first contact or visit to discharge or recovery. (This is the sum of all process steps and waiting times.)
7. Compare your current value stream map with your ideal value stream.
8. Design your future state value stream; your target condition (see Figure 9.3 for an example of a possible future state of the value stream from Figure 9.2).
9. Make a plan for how you will realize the target condition; your future value stream.

---

[2] Take time is the rhythm of customer demand and tells how often a patient needs to be helped. You calculate the takt time by dividing your available time (for example: eight hours per day) by the number of patients who need to use the care process during that period (for example eight per day). The takt time in this case is eight hours divided by eight patients = one hour. If your process (step) takes longer than one hour you know your process can't keep up with demand and waiting times will arise.

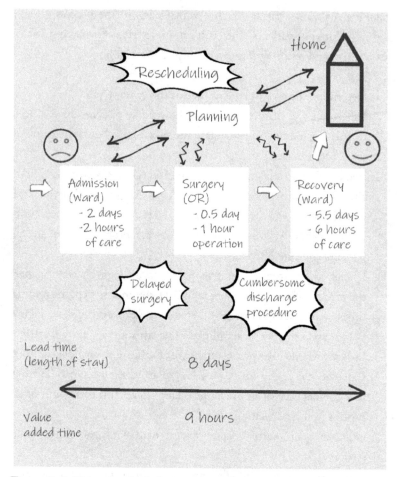

Figure 9.2 Example of a value stream map (current state)

You use the value stream map to visualize the current state and to design your future state, your improved value stream, or—in other words—your target condition. Based on this you make an improvement plan that presents the steps you are going to take and the improvements you need to make to realize the future state value stream.

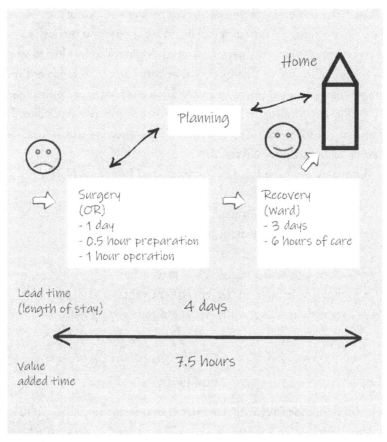

Figure 9.3 Example of a value stream map (future state)

Key Performance Indicators (KPIs)

In order to monitor the progress and direction of your improvement process you need indicators. As the name suggests indicators give an indication of whether something is changing and in which direction. This can be both on process level (how much time does something take) and on result level (Were you on time?). During an improvement process you want to know how you are performing—are you ahead or behind?

Be aware however that you don't need to know everything. Focus on the core of your improvement process and make sure you use metrics to give you a prediction whether you are on the right track. Just like in your car where indicators in a navigation system and on your dashboard tell you whether you are going to be successful in reaching your destination.

Performance indicators will help best when you derive them directly from True North so they help you monitor the direction that is ideal for your patients and other stakeholders.

Examples of performance indicators derived from True North:

- Number of safety incidents (target = 0).
- Number of re-admissions (target = 0).
- Waiting times (target = 0).
- Patient satisfaction (target = 100 percent).
- Employee satisfaction (target = 100 percent)
- Productivity (target = 100 percent of time adding value)

Focus[3]

A pitfall that leaders regularly tend to fall into is thinking that ambition is determined by the amount of goals and projects they want to achieve over a period of time. They equate ambition with effort. The more goals and projects the better you get.

Experience shows however that in that case you are mainly busy with the other project and are spending a lot of time determining what you are going to work on next over and over again. By constantly changing goals and projects you lose a lot of time and attention. It also leads to confusion because often it is not clear what the most important thing is and when you are being successful. When everything is finished?

You should provide focus so that all energy and initiatives go in the same direction. If you can focus your attention on one thing for a longer period of time you will achieve much better and more creative results. You also avoid wasting time and talent because people don't have to worry

---

[3] Orelio 2021, Chapter 12.

about what the goals are and managing projects instead of realizing them. Focus also helps to keep the momentum going.

Avoid Suboptimization[4]

One of the most difficult things is to keep the various interests of the various parties in balance. When making your plans make sure you know all the stakeholders and which things they value. Then define the problem you want to solve from these different perspectives and if possible, include each of the parties in your improvement process. This is necessary to avoid suboptimization.[5] This requires a system analysis so that everyone's contribution and importance can be identified but above all to arrive at a common vision and consensus about the problem you want to solve. In this way you organize balance and support among all parties at the front end.

For your key performance indicators (KPIs), this means that you monitor your performance in various areas. For example, safety, quality, service, productivity, and teamwork. Doing this you monitor the interests of patients, employees, and management in a limited set of performance indicators while the focus is on patients and added value being delivered. You may notice that there are no financial indicators between them. When you score well on all these aspects then your financial performance will also be in order. However, you only know your financial performance in retrospect and financial performance indicators are therefore not suitable for the daily management of your process.

Balance Your Time

By now you understand that focus and balance are important. However, if you examine your own calendar and all the things you have to do I imagine it's all rather overwhelming. Maybe you think: "How do I make

---

[4] Orelio 2021, Chapter 12.

[5] Suboptimization means an improvement for one is making it worse for another. As a consequence, the overall system is not improving.

time to do all this?" Especially if you're just starting out or if your department is mainly firefighting. Where do you start then?

At Boeing, the same problem occurred. The employees on the floor were mainly troubleshooting while the management was mainly following their daily standards and routines being busy with each other in meetings. They found out that in order to achieve structural improvements they had to literally reverse roles: the employees on the shop floor—the mechanics—needed standards in order to deliver quality consistently and efficiently while management needed to lead improvements (with and for the mechanics) and to stimulate innovation (see Figure 9.4 for this shift in roles and the resulting time spent on standard work versus improving and innovating).

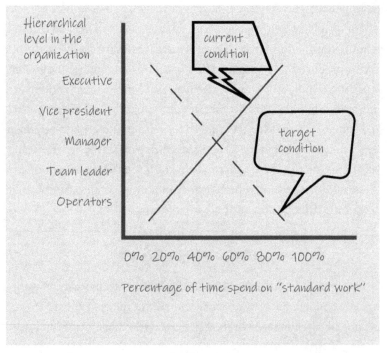

Figure 9.4 Time spent on standard work versus improvement

The answer to the question "Where do I start?" is simple but not easy—as it was for Boeing. First, you look for problems (see Chapter 4). Then you start your improvement process by removing overburden and standardize the processes and ways of working in your team (see

Chapter 5). Ensure that care providers can carry out most of their work safely, correctly, efficiently, and routinely. In other words, stabilize your team and the care processes. This brings peace and saves them and you a lot of time. Many of the fires you won't have to "fight." This allows the care providers to spend more time and attention on their patients. Your calendar will open up to spend more time and attention on your team.

When your team and processes are stable you start looking for structural improvement of your processes. You will work from small to large. Meaning that you start with individual tasks and actions you and your team can improve directly without any investment. The more experience you gain the bigger the processes you improve. The bigger and more complex the problems you tackle the deeper (in traditional words: higher) in the organization the responsibility lies to make sure they are solved. In a learning organization the responsibility for a problem is placed as low as possible in the organization at the highest necessary level.

Ultimately you strive for a time distribution at the different levels in the organization as shown in Figure 9.4, which can be seen as the ideal and the guideline for your change process. You can use it as a touchstone for daily reality and as a source of inspiration for the target condition of your calendar and that of your colleagues.

Student's Thoughts

1. What process do you use to develop and communicate your vision, objectives, and plans?
2. How many different goals do you have? How many different projects are you working on?
3. For which stakeholders do your goals and projects deliver improvement?
4. How do you know if you are actually moving toward your goal?
5. To which value stream(s) does your team belong?
6. What is your vision of your value stream's future state?
7. What is your improvement plan to move toward that future state?
8. How is your time divided between standard work, improvement, and innovation?
9. How would you like it to be distributed?

CHAPTER 10

Why Change Is So Hard?!

Do you want
change?

Yes!

Do you want
to change?

No!

Figure 10.1 (To) change?!

Improvement is a change process toward the goal. And improvement that's what everyone is just in favor of! Starting with Lean to achieve improvements is therefore very popular. Especially the idea that you are going to use your common sense to do your work and to improve appeals to many. Until it becomes clear that it is not about improvement but about improving continuously. Because that means changing (your own behavior) continuously (Figure 10.1).

Change starts with a concrete need or a concrete problem, which makes change necessary. It is important that before you start you have this need clear and are motivated. Your motivation depends on many things such as safety, conviction, and being open to and trusting in change.

Lean requires a different way of thinking. Certainly, at the moment when Lean thinking requires a long-term perspective while the short-term screams for a solution, resistance can arise. Resistance is where your thinking (vision, values, assumptions) does not correspond with the reality that presents itself. This results in the most important task you have as a leader of change: "Chief Barrier Remover." All obstacles that stand in the way of people to change you will have to (help) remove one by one (Orelio 2021, Chapter 13).

Chain of Successful Change

The chain of successful change (see Figure 10.2) is a tool to test whether you have considered the most important elements of your change process. When one of the links in the chain is missing you will experience a specific form of resistance. This resistance is a signal that something is still missing or can be improved in the change process and the way you are leading it. Do assume that the problem (read: the resistance) is not the individual's fault but is caused by the process you are using. So, don't blame yourself either but learn from it and adapt your process (Orelio 2021, Chapter 11).

Vision

In previous chapters you have read that giving direction is one of the most important tasks of a leader. "If you don't know where you want to go it doesn't matter which path you take," said the cat from *Alice in*

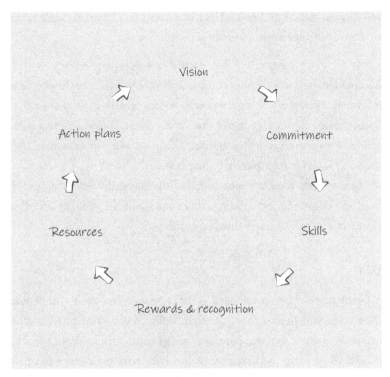

Vision

Action plans

Commitment

Resources

Skills

Rewards & recognition

Figure 10.2 Chain of successful change

Wonderland. So, for your change process to succeed it's essential that everyone knows where you're going and why.

If that is clear then everyone can help and support each other. Therefore, make sure you formulate the goal of your change—your vision—in such a way that it gives a concrete, recognizable, and inspiring image of the future. This makes it possible for everyone to move toward the vision together and to be enthusiastic about it.

Communicate your vision at every opportunity and start every meeting or conversation with it. "To be successful you will have to communicate your vision 10,000 times more often than you think," change management guru John Kotter said (Kotter 1996).

Commitment

Just having a vision is certainly not enough for a successful change. The effect of your change is not only determined by the quality of the change you have in mind but above all by the support you have managed to create among the people you impact with your change.

In a formula: Effect = Quality × Acceptance^2.
Acceptance weighs more heavily (quadratically) because people who commit themselves to the changes will help you to achieve the right—high—quality when the quality is too low. When there is low acceptance the quality does not really matter because then you will almost certainly not realize the change (completely or permanently).

You achieve acceptance or support for change by involving people from the beginning, by building consensus about the problem and your vision and by working together on solutions.

Skills

A factor that is often overlooked is that people who have to implement the change will need to have the right skills. If you don't provide them you make them insecure. Leaders of change usually think about the skills needed to perform the new process but only after the change has been implemented. So, people don't learn beforehand what exactly is going to change and why. It is not enough to have skills for performing the new process. If you want people to learn to solve their own problems and thus improve their processes themselves then people will also have to develop problem solving, improvement, and change management skills. For example, you will have to teach people to work together, communicate, give feedback, and experiment. The ultimate goal of continuous improvement is after all that people continuously improve and develop themselves and their leadership thus increasing the learning, problem solving, and innovative capacity of the organization.

Rewards and Recognition

A very effective way to motivate and stimulate people—which is often overlooked—is to show appreciation. When you let people know that you are happy with their contribution and efforts you make them feel that they are valuable. In this way you stimulate people to show the behavior you want more often.

Rewarding people is most effective when you give them personal appreciation. Attention and positive feedback—from colleagues or executives—are much more important to people than a monetary reward. This is because money is a dissatisfier. Money makes people dissatisfied when it is not there but does not provide much extra motivation when it is there.

As a result, when people are financially insecure or unclear about their exact income, they will optimize their income rather than their processes and performances.[1] Therefore, do not link your improvement process to monetary rewards. Express your appreciation for people's creativity and efforts. Reward them by listening to them, by implementing their ideas swiftly and handing them a stage to show their improvements. Celebrating successes is a great way to show appreciation and stimulate people to keep on improving.

Resources

Little is as frustrating for people as being asked to come up with ideas for improvement but not being given the means to actually realize their ideas. This is an important reason for people to drop out. As a leader you will therefore need to think about how much time and money you are willing to invest. Clarity in advance creates a framework and makes it clear to people what they can expect from you.

When it comes to process improvements be a bit stingy when it comes to budget because you want to use people's creativity instead of throwing money at it. An additional problem is that the care providers usually do not have the authority to decide on large amounts of money, which slows down the improvement process because they first have to ask for permission. You can also put the responsibility and authority for the budget and for spending money lower down in the organization—closer to the shop floor. In this way you give confidence and avoid bureaucracy and lengthy processes.

---

[1] For this reason, you need to ensure that the decisions that healthcare providers make on behalf of patients are not directly related to the level of their income.

Another problem with spending money to improve is that in order to be able to make up a budget you need to be aware of the measures you are going to take. You may end up in a process in which management does the thinking and will make the decisions while there is no direct involvement of care providers and no good, factual analysis of the current condition. This is disastrous for the support and effectiveness of the improvement plans made.

Challenge people by asking them, "How could you improve your work for patients today without investment?" You'll be amazed at what is possible.

Action Plans

Being too eager to change everything without informing people about what is going to happen will make you look like a loose cannon. In order to avoid starting off on the wrong foot and taking unnecessary risks you need an action plan. Not having a plan is a risk because you don't know exactly what is going to happen. Your plan is your reference point to know whether you make things worse instead of better. It is your guide and support for learning and adjusting.

However, it is wasteful to have an overly comprehensive and detailed plan containing all the steps you expect to take well into the future to reach your final goal. Such a plan suggests that you know exactly what to do, when to do it, and what obstacles you are going to encounter. It suggests that you can predict the future. Furthermore, an extensive plan takes a lot of time to make and all that time you don't actually take action and you don't learn anything. Like a famous boxer once said, "Your plan is true until the first punch in the face!"

So how do you make an action plan that works and helps you? Your action plan describes who is going to take action, what results you expect from this, when we can see what the real effect is, and what we can to learn from it. In this way you remove obstacle by obstacle on your way to your goal. Based on what you learn you adjust your plan if necessary and determine your next step. So, you follow the PDCA learning cycle in which you always look one step ahead, on your way to your goal.

Communication

Up until now I have always urged you in this book to involve people, to share your vision, and spend a lot of time and energy on imaging. These are all forms of communication and the core of your change process. Communication is a difficult but also one of the most important elements that you can control. Your own way of communication is therefore an important and necessary part of your personal development plan. Make sure you learn what your preferred styles and pitfalls are when communicating with others. Also solicit feedback from other people you communicate with.

A lot can go wrong in personal communication between people. For clarity in your communication make use of visualization and assure that everyone can see at a glance what the standards and objectives are and what's actually happening. This saves you a lot of time, energy, and (mis) communication and most importantly it helps people to do the right thing.

Individual Obstacles and Struggles[2]

In order to understand, apply and learn new ways—such as the Lean way—everyone goes through their own processes. Keep in mind that nothing changes automatically. Everyone has their own qualities, pitfalls, and learning styles. Resistance is a natural part of people's learning processes. People will feel uncomfortable when they have to go beyond their knowledge thresholds and outside their comfort zones.

When you are the learner it will require discipline, determination, and optimism to learn the new ways. Keep developing yourself despite feeling uncomfortable. For it is a signal from the brain that it is working hard and learning new patterns. Think of this as good news and not as a reason to stop because it "doesn't suit you." Keep remembering that you are doing it to develop and improve yourself.

When you are the coach it will require patience and the awareness that resistance is part of the learning process. Again, blame the process

---

[2] Orelio 2021, Chapter 11.

and not the person. When the learning process stagnates first consider how you can improve the learning and change process by identifying the causes of the stagnation. Do not project the stagnation onto an entire group, "The team is not making progress."

Successful Change Starts and Ends with Leadership

The process of change seems to be mainly about others and how to deal with and communicate with them, for example, when they show resistance. If you look at it this way you are getting a hard time changing anything. It is more effective when you see change as being mainly about yourself and the process of leadership that you apply. How do you react to people? What do you do when you yourself are resisting certain parts of the change? How do you tackle the obstacles that stand in your way of realizing your vision? How are you helping other people to remove their obstacles?

Change management is also process management: The right process gives the right results. If you don't succeed in changing something successfully it's not other people's mistake. Find the causes for the lack of success in the process of leadership and change that you apply. Analyze the process, learn from it, and adjust, for example, change your behavior or your own way of thinking.

One of the most common barriers to being a successful leader are the assumptions you have about how the world works. Just regularly research and test your assumptions to see which thoughts are hampering progress.

What Didn't Work?

Time and again I have tried to achieve continuous improvement together with my clients based on Lean principles. And though it's hard to admit: it wasn't always a success. There are some pitfalls—which people keep on falling into as I have done. What can we learn from that? I encountered three major pitfalls (Orelio 2021, Chapter 14).

Pitfall 1: Seeing Lean as a Set of Improvement Tools

At the first introduction to Lean the methods, the tools, and techniques are the visible change. But these are no more than an effective way to make problems visible and understandable. Methods and techniques themselves, however, do not change people's mindset and behavior. This is much more determined by how you use the tools and how you deal with people.

Pitfall 2: Implementing Lean by Sending People on Training

Giving people knowledge about Lean is not so much a wrong step, but it's just the very beginning of the change process. It helps to raise awareness and develop a common language, but it is not enough to actually achieve continuous improvement. This requires daily practice and coaching. Training alone does not change mindsets and behaviors. People move on to the order of the day fairly quickly after the training. Certainly, as long as they are being managed in the old way.

Pitfall 3: Wanting to Convince Others

It is very tempting to use one's own belief in Lean to convince others so that they also want to work with it. Use your conviction and belief in the Lean principles not for others but for yourself. Apply the principles to your own work and develop yourself in this way. By showing others your new way, they may become inspired and stimulated to experiment and improve their own work based on Lean principles.

Student's Thoughts

1. What process are you going to follow in order to successfully realize your desired changes?
2. What role do you have in that process?
3. How are you going to find out if you have included all aspects of the *chain of successful change* in your approach?
4. What pitfalls do you foresee? What measures will you take to avoid them?
5. How do you deal with your own resistance?

CHAPTER 11

Case Study: Successful Standardization through Job Instruction (JI)

In response to one of my columns (Orelio 2018) people from the Leiden University Hospital—LUMC—told me that unlike many other hospitals they meet little to no resistance when it comes to standardization. In their hospital they see enthusiasm. Enthusiasm for standardization? I could hardly believe it. In my experience standardization is one of the more controversial topics when you talk about continuous improvement, Lean healthcare, and its origins at Toyota. People quickly think that standardization kills creativity and the idea is that you have to do your work for patients like robots on an assembly line. Nothing could be further from the truth as LUMC proves.

LUMC is an academic medical center in Leiden, the Netherlands, whose core tasks are patient care, research, and medical education. Patient care mainly concerns care in life-threatening situations and highly specialized care for which special, often advanced, knowledge and equipment are required.

In 2010 LUMC started a process of continuous improvement based on Lean principles. As part of their approach a team of Lean coaches was formed that teach people in the organization how to improve their processes.

Unfortunately, also in LUMC the correct execution of nursing tasks is not always successful. For example, people perform actions in different ways, skip steps, or perform them incorrectly. This can lead to quality and safety problems for both patients and caregivers.

To counter this, one of their goals was to improve the way of working at the Acute Admissions Department. The approach used at that time was not successful. When their Lean coaches became acquainted with Training Within Industries (TWI) and more specifically with the Job Instruction (JI) component, they immediately realized that this could help them to successfully improve their working methods (see Chapter 5).

In situations where mistakes are made, we are quickly inclined to ask questions such as, "Why did you make this mistake?" "Why don't people just do what they need to do?" But not in LUMC. Just as in the Lean philosophy their starting point is that problems do not lie with the individual care providers but with the system in which they work. Think of people who have had different educators or training courses or people who forget something because they are in a hurry or simply because it is a long time ago since they performed that procedure. It also happens that people develop their own approach based on their experiences in the workplace and the problems they personally encounter.

Job Instruction (JI) has been developed for these situations. JI helps to prevent mistakes by standardizing working methods and training everyone in the same way so that the best conceivable way becomes routine (Graupp and Purrier 2012). When something becomes a routine people don't know any better and will perform their work in the right way over and over again automatically. It is also much more noticeable when someone deviates, which allows colleagues to help each other, give feedback, and learn from each other.

But how do you introduce a new method like JI for a hospital? And how do you organize it in such a way that it becomes a permanent part of your way of working?

Like all other innovations the introduction of JI in LUMC is a process of continuous learning and improvement. Don't see this case as a roadmap for successful implementation of JI but as an example of a certain approach and what you can learn from it. While reading it you should realize that the change process is at least as important as the standardization process itself.

A Characteristic Result of JI: The Infusion Needle

A good example of the impact that JI can have can be seen in the introduction of new infusion needles in the obstetrics department of LUMC, "the house of birth." With the introduction of the new infusion needle no one except for a few nurses actually managed to insert the infusion needles correctly the first time despite the instructions of the supplier. There were even calls to stop using the new needles.

Until—with the help of JI—they had made an analysis of the task of applying the new needle and developed, recorded, and trained it in the correct way. In particular the improved dexterity of nurses ensured that they injected the needle first time right. After everyone had been trained on the basis of the new JI by the Job Instructors hardly any mistakes were reported. These and other applications made not only the nurses involved enthusiastic about JI but also colleagues from other disciplines and departments. As a result, people started to demand standardization and training of other tasks while using JI. This created an organic spread of JI.

Nurses in the Lead

It is nice to see that this approach provides a way for nurses and other care providers to show leadership. They now have a way to improve the quality of care by directly tackling variations in working methods themselves. This produces impressive results, which also helps them to make their colleagues enthusiastic.

Nursing craftsmanship is paramount here. Due to the highly standardized and well-founded working methods there are little to no reasons to be against it. The effect of this bottom-up movement is that more and more colleagues ask voluntarily whether the Job Instructor can train them.

Tasks that can be done better—for example because they potentially endanger the patient—are now immediately improved by nurses themselves. On the basis of Job Instruction (JI), they jointly develop an improved standard way of working that can be quickly spread to all colleagues involved. During the introduction of new devices, they now have a method to work in the best possible way right from the start: safely, correctly, and efficiently.

In this case it is about nurses, but there are similar experiences in other departments and disciplines such as the facilities department.

Train, Train, Train

At the start of the implementation of JI, the LUMC Job Instructors were trained by the TWI Institute in the Netherlands to ensure that they would start implementing JI with the right trainer, the right skills, and methodical principles. Next they trained two internal JI trainers. These internal JI trainers now train their colleagues to become Job Instructors. There is currently[1] a total of 47 active Job Instructors. These Job Instructors have trained hundreds of people in the various tasks that people need to master.

The training (read: Job Instruction) always takes place in the departments—often in specially equipped rooms—so that the work situation of the task to be trained is imitated as realistically as possible. JI is on-the-job training. The Job Instructors take care of the training plan, the task analyses, and giving training to colleagues.

The Job Instructors are organized as a kind of network. They come together once every two weeks to share learning experiences, to inform each other about the progress in the departments, to ask questions, and to offer support for example in making task analyses. These biweekly meetings are highly appreciated and especially the support in making task analyses are seen as a real added value of the network.

In order to keep the network on the right track a Core Team of JI has been formed at LUMC consisting of five members: two JI trainers and three Job Instructors. They ensure that the necessary fine-tuning, preparation, administration, and planning run smoothly. In addition, the JI Core Team is also responsible for the training of (new) Job Instructors.

All this turns out to require a surprising amount of effort and coordination. Think of planning, organizing, and preparing the network meetings, arranging the necessary spaces, registering participants, and working out minutes, among other things. This while most Job Instructors would prefer to just perform Job Instructions. Especially because they have to do it on the side because they also have their own work—as nurses for example. Arranging it all goes in between regular tasks.

---

[1] The number of Job Instructors within the LUMC mentioned here was the number at the time of my observations and interviews, May 2019.

The Training Matrix

An effective way to increase employee involvement and make the training process run efficiently is making progress visible through visual management. For example, at LUMC a training matrix has been created in the form of a board—made out of Legos—to get an overview of whether all employees have been trained. You can see at a glance on the training matrix who needs to be trained and when so that the Job Instructor can make a training plan.

The columns of the training matrix contain the tasks that need to be trained and the rows contain the names of the employees in the respective department or team. On the training matrix the training status of each task—per employee—is indicated in colors. Yellow means "yet to be trained," green means "trained," and black means "does not need to be trained."

The training matrix is part of the daily team huddle. If the Job Instructor is present the team will discuss the training matrix. In the photograph (Figure 11.1) you see a team huddle and on the left a training matrix.

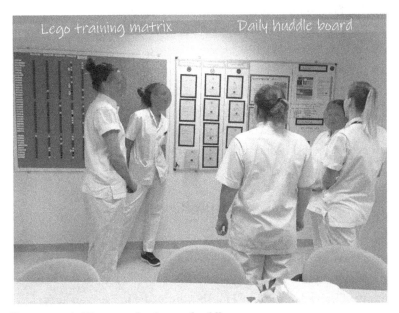

Figure 11.1 Photograph of team huddle

Task Analysis

When there is a need to train a certain task with JI this will be announced in the network meeting. The Job Instructors discuss the task and examine whether there may be people who already have experience with it. If it has been decided to set up a JI training for the task then the first step is a task analysis.

A task analysis is a careful process by a team of people involved in which you divide the task to be trained into its different steps and determine the correct order of these steps. The emphasis is on the important steps that actually move the task forward. The task analysis is primarily intended to train people in the right way and is therefore primarily intended as a tool for the Job Instructor.

At LUMC they carry out the task analysis in multidisciplinary teams of, for example, nurses, service staff, and hospital hygienists. The composition of this team depends on the task they are going to instruct. It brings different disciplines closer together. It creates an understanding for each other's profession and needs, which makes working methods much more compatible. This multidisciplinary collaboration is perhaps the most important effect of the implementation of JI. Different disciplines together focus on the process needed to care for patients.

The team decides on the basis of consensus what the (new) standard will be. Consensus is reached when they dare to say, "This is currently the best possible way to carry out this task. For now, this is the standard and the basis for further improvement."

In addition to standardizing existing working methods LUMC also applies JI to the introduction of new processes or devices. JI helps them to develop the best conceivable standard from the outset and to train everyone accordingly.

Dealing with Resistance

Although I have attended a workshop at the TWI Institute, I never have experienced what it is like to be trained by a Job Instructor myself. At LUMC I was given this opportunity. The special thing was that being an outsider I learned to perform a nursing procedure in half an hour: analyzing the blood of an unborn baby using the iScan.

I was quite nervous beforehand—just as I was during the exam for my typing course in high school—the big difference being that during the JI training I was confident within 30 minutes and maybe even proud of my new skill, while I never got my typing degree.

In retrospect the JI training reminded me very much of the resuscitation course I had taken. It seems to be based on the same principles. After the training we put my experience next to that of the Job Instructors. After all I am also a trainer, so we shared the struggle with the resistances of the participants and how you deal with them. Resistances that I myself had just partly experienced personally during my training.

Resistance type one: "JI is like school." This resistance seems to occur especially in adults. They are no longer accustomed to school methods of training. Usually the courses and training or the congresses you attend are noncommittal. You can decide for yourself if and how you learn. During a JI training the trainer determines how you learn namely with the world's best method. And not learning is not an option. So, it is important that you make this clear to people beforehand and put them at ease. That is the first step of JI.

Resistance type two: "Being trained is uncomfortable and this method is not for me." This form of resistance resembles the first one but is slightly different because it only occurs when you actually get to work. The resistance is directed at the new way in which a task has to be performed. Here too the trainer will have to take the resistance seriously, but he should not bow to it because then people will continue to do it in their own old way.

Feeling uncomfortable is inevitable if you are going to learn new things. As said before it requires extra effort from the brain, which then resists by making you feel uncomfortable. Our brains are constantly busy dealing with using energy as efficiently as possible and a learning process is by definition not efficient.

You can prepare the trainee for this by explaining that feeling uncomfortable is part of the process and it is a sign that you are learning. It is also important that you stand up for your approach. In order to prevent problems and resistances later in the training process the trainer can agree in advance that the method you apply is not up for discussion. After all it is the best method you—as a trainer—know for this application, it is your profession.

The Role of Team Leaders and Managers

The most important tasks that LUMC Job Instructors see for executives and management are facilitating and supporting. They want managers to free up time and resources so that the Job Instructors can train everyone who wants or needs to be trained. They would also like management to support administrative and coordinating tasks. The commitment of the managers is not yet as strong in all of them but it is growing. This is important for the further spread of JI.

Although TWI—and therefore also JI—has team leaders as its primary target group at LUMC it is still up to the team leaders themselves how they deal with it. At the beginning of the implementation process of JI this varied from resistance to the method to extremely enthusiastic team leaders who are Job Instructors themselves. Meanwhile all team leaders are open to it although some see barriers and are sometimes not equally enthusiastic. They sometimes wonder: "How do I make JI successful in my department?" It is up to the managers—supported by a Lean coach or a JI coordinator—to help team leaders to answer these kinds of questions and to help them remove the barriers in the way of a successful implementation of JI.

Spreading the New Way of Working

If you want to disseminate a new method such as Job Instruction it requires the conviction of the people involved that it will actually help them. Therefore, start the introduction of the new method in a safe environment where you form a collective vision of the problems you want to solve, the urgency of this, and the positive impact the new method will have on your problems.

In LUMC the Job Instructors are healthcare professionals (mainly nurses but also doctors, assistants, pharmacist's assistants, sterilization service staff, and hospital hygienists) and some team leaders (nurses and service staff). The JI Trainers are a pediatric nurse and a Lean Coach (formerly surgery nurse). Together with the other Job Instructors they are now the owners of the method and its spread across the organization.

This has its limitations because they have relatively little influence on other disciplines or departments such as doctors. They mainly try to convince colleagues of the value of Job Instruction with their enthusiasm and by showing results. The multidisciplinary approach chosen by LUMC in which the task (and not the organizational structure) determines who participates provides an easily accessible way to get acquainted with Job Instruction. This makes it very effective in spreading it across departments and disciplines without any hierarchical power.

In order to convince more colleagues and managers more will probably be needed in the future than the enthusiasm of the proponents of JI. Questions such as, "What problem do we solve with this?" "Why is this important?" "What do my patients and I gain from this?" will probably have to be answered.

That's why the Job Instructors are busy talking to other departments and disciplines, answering their questions and sharing their insights and results achieved in order to spread JI not only organically but also in a structured way within LUMC and beyond.

Do you want to create a movement from within just like in LUMC? Start with the people who want it. Their examples, positive reactions, and the attention they get will then help to persuade doubters in your group. At this stage ignore the real opponents until you have created a sufficient group of believers.

Connection to the Goals of the Organization

For further commitment and involvement of senior management you need to connect the possibilities of the new method with the goals of the organization. In this way you make it clear to managers how JI helps them to achieve their goals.

When they gain this insight, it is easier for them to take responsibility for the implementation and dissemination of JI. Like other people they first want to be convinced of the positive impact of Job Instruction as a method of achieving their goals.

A good example in LUMC of linking the organizational goals to the possibilities of JI are the instructions given by Job Instructors in the field of hand hygiene and the putting on and taking off of protective clothing, which are among the most important ways to avoid hospital-acquired infections. So, these instructions link the application of JI directly to one of the LUMC's hospital wide objectives: prevention of hospital-acquired infections.

Another development that links the organization's objectives directly to Job Instruction is that the Job Instructors are increasingly considering using JI to instruct patients and informal caretakers prior to their discharge from hospital. Using JI, you could give each patient or informal caretaker a standardized and high-quality instruction, which will help them to remain independent for as long as possible, leading to less need for home care and more autonomy, control, and freedom.

Sustaining the Gains

Although sustainment is last mentioned, it does require attention from the beginning of a change process like the implementation and spread of Job Instruction. With sustainment we mean that you make sure that:

1. the approach is anchored in the organization in such a way that it is part of "how we do things around here" and the application is not dependent on a few individuals and
2. the results achieved are retained in order to be able to improve them further.

At LUMC sustainment takes place at the following levels:

- The *employees* who have been trained. For this purpose, LUMC is still looking for the right way to test whether they are carrying out the trained tasks correctly in everyday practice. This is still work in progress. However, they do test whether common tasks are executed in the right way—when a new skill is learned—of which the previously trained skill is a part. For example, "hand disinfection" is part of the task "taking off protective clothing."

This could be extended to organizing observations at the workplace of already trained colleagues in order to determine whether they manage to continue to perform the trained task correctly. And if not to investigate why. This could result in extra training or improved task analysis.

- The *Job Instructors* themselves: Will they continue to do the tasks and skills of the Job Instructor properly? To answer this question LUMC uses peer reviews. Once a year the Job Instructor is assessed by a colleague Job Instructor on how to perform a Job Instruction. They also assess each other annually on making a task analysis. Do they still do that as they should? This assessment takes place during master classes organized by the JI Core Team. The training matrix is audited periodically during the coaching interviews that each department (Team Leader and Job Instructors) has with two JI Core Team members.

In my opinion there is a third level of sustainment to be distinguished: the *management system*. After all it is a management responsibility to ensure that everyone—ultimately—participates and adheres to the standards. For a structured and sustained spread you will have to make the new method part of the management system or—in other words—part of the standard arsenal of standardization and improvement methods.

This requires that executives and managers understand the method (principles and details) before they (can) lead JI spreading. Therefore, you should include them in the (first) Job Instructor training groups. The more managers are enthusiastic and involved in the dissemination the less dependent you are on the change skills of a small group of leaders for success.

To assure sustainment of JI you should develop methods for frequent assessments of the trained tasks in daily practice and pay a lot of attention to the change process required for successful implementation and spread of JI. It will certainly help to make the results you achieve with

Job Instruction visible and tangible so you can convince more and more people of the added value of this fantastic method.

JI as the Answer to Staff Shortages?

In addition to the substantive impact of Job Instruction on improving quality and safety in LUMC it also has a very positive effect on the employees. It brings them together, gives them energy, and enables people to improve their work for patients by themselves.

Through research by a student from Erasmus University—in the transplant department of LUMC—we now also know that JI has a positive effect on team dynamics. People feel safer, which makes talking about work—especially if you have done something wrong—easier and less scary.

In these times of staff shortages, it is very important to be an attractive employer. Retaining staff and attracting new employees are among LUMC's most important objectives. Here too JI seems to be making a substantial, positive contribution.

Student's Thoughts

1. What do you think is the essence of this case?
2. What do you learn from this case about Lean? Standardization? Successful change? Leadership? Your own role in this?
3. What action could you take yourself tomorrow to improve your own situation based on these lessons?
4. What ideas do you have that would help LUMC?

CHAPTER 12

Action Plans: Improve in Small Steps—Learning Is the Goal

If you think that you're too small to make a difference try sleeping in a closed room with a mosquito.

—African proverb

After reading this book maybe you will think, "Alright but now I want to go to work and what exactly am I going to do first?" In order to answer this question, the following action plan has been drawn up, consisting of two phases.

Phase 1: Develop Yourself as a Leader[1]

1. Go to the workplace—your area of responsibility—and start observing and understanding the current work and how it is done.
2. Make problems visible.
3. Start by tackling those problems you are experiencing yourself.
4. Think of countermeasures you can take yourself—today—while not spending money.
5. Reflect on each step.
6. Record your lessons and results and share them with your colleagues.
7. Keep going—with the help of a coach—and keep developing yourself.

---

[1] Orelio 2021, Chapter 15.

Phase 2: Involve Your Team and Coach Them

8. Start every day with a morning meeting. Possible agenda:
   a. Discuss the performance.
   b. Talk about mistakes and how to avoid them.
   c. Learn from the previous day or shift.
   d. Prepare the coming day or shift.
   e. Ask for improvement ideas.
   f. Let people present their improvements (at their work place).
9. Free up five minutes each day for sweeping, sorting, and standardizing ($3S^2$). Everyone participates and especially the leader.
10. Free up another five minutes each day in which people—in small groups—train each other in skills and practices that are important for their work.
11. Develop your leader standard work (LSW) based on the needs of your team.
12. Keep going, coach them, keep developing them ...

Student's Thoughts

This action plan is only a suggestion. Determine what you are actually going to do based on where you are in your personal development and what your team or department needs, in that order.

Pay attention! What a team needs is often not the same as what the team is asking for.

The only remaining question now is, "What will be your first step"?

I wish you a lot of success and fun while you are continuously improving (yourself)!

---

[2] 3S has been derived from 5S: a lean method to establish a safe and efficient work environment (Akers 2012).

References

Akers, P. 2012. *2 Second Lean. How to Grow People and Build a Fun Lean Culture. At Work & at Home*. 2nd Edition. Bellingham, WA: FastCap Press.

Argyris, C., and D. Schon. 1974. *Theory in Practice: Increasing Professional Effectiveness*. San Francisco, SF: Jossey Bass.

Garcia, H. 2017. *Ikigai: The Japanese secret to a Long and Happy Life*. London, UK: Hutchinson.

Goldsmith, M. 2007. Feed Forward, https://marshallgoldsmith.com/articles/1438/.

Graban, M. 2018. *Measures of Success: React Less, Lead Better, Improve More*. Colleyville: Constancy, Inc.

Graupp, J., and M. Purrier. 2012. *Getting to Standard Work in Healthcare: Using TWI to Create a Foundation for Quality Care*. Boca Raton: Productivity Press.

Harada, T., and N. Bodek. 2012. *The Harada Method. The Spirit of Self-Reliance*. Vancouver: WA. PCS Press.

Hattie, J., and S. Clarke. 2018. *Visual Learning. Feedback*. Abingdon-on-Thames: Routledge.

Keller, G., and J. Papasan. 2014. *The One Thing. The Surprisingly Simple Truth Behind Extraordinary Results*. London, UK: John Murray.

Kenney, C. 2011. *Transforming Healthcare. Virginia Mason Medical Center's Pursuit of the Perfect Patient Experience*. Boca Raton, FL: CRC Press.

Kotter, J. 1996. *Leading Change*. Boston: Harvard Business School Press.

Laarman, B.S., R.J. Bouwman, A.J. de Veer, and R.D. Friele. 2019. "How do Doctors in the Netherlands Perceive the Impact of Disciplinary Procedures and Disclosure of Disciplinary Measures on their Professional Practice, Health and Career Opportunities? A Questionnaire Among Medical Doctors Who Received a Disciplinary Measure." *BMJ Open* 9, no. 3, p. e023576. doi: 10.1136/bmjopen-2018-023576

Liker, J. 2004. *The Toyota Way. 14 Management Principles from the World's Greatest Manufacturer*. New York City, NY: McGraw-Hill Education.

Liker, J., and G. Convis. 2012. *The Toyota Way to Lean Leadership. Achieving and Sustaining Excellence through Leadership Development*. United States of America: Mcgraw-Hill.

Luttik, K. 2011. *Standaarden voor leidinggeven*. Amsterdam: Symposium lean zorg 25 mrt '11, VUmc.

Ohno, T. 1988. *Toyota Production System. Beyond Large-Scale Production*. New York, NY: Productivity Press.

Orelio, A. 2018. *Toyota*. OK Visie Krant Nr., p. 15, www.okvisie.nl

Orelio, A. 2019. *Mensen Beter Maken. Veilig, met compassie, zonder verspilling, geen gedoe*. Utrecht: Stili Novi.

Orelio, A. 2021. *Lean Thinking in Healthcare: Safe, Compassionate, Zero Waste, No Struggle*. Utrecht: Stili Novi.

Pereira, R. 2014. *One Piece Flow vs. Mass Production Envelope Stuffing. Lean Thinking Simulation*. Gemba Academy. https://youtube.com/watch?v=Dr67i5SdXiM

Pink, D.H. 2009. *Drive. The Surprising Truth About What Motivates Us*. New York, NY: Riverhead Books.

Rother, M., and J. Shook. 1999. *Learning to See. Value Stream Mapping to Add Value and Eliminate Muda*. Boston, MA: Lean Enterprise Institute.

Rother, M. 2010. *The Toyota Kata. Managing People for Improvement, Adaptiveness and Superior Results*. United States of America: Mcgraw-Hill.

Shook, J. 2010. *Managing to Learn. Using the A3 Management Process to Solve Problems, Gain Agreement, Mentor, and Lead*. Driebergen: Lean Management Institute.

Smalley, A. 2018. *Four Types of Problems. From Reactive Troubleshooting to Creative Innovation*. Boston MA: Lean Enterprise Institute Inc.

Spear, S., H. Bowen, and H. Kent. 1999. "Decoding the DNA of the Toyota Production System". *Harvard Business Review* 77, 96–108.

Tiggelaar, B. 2009. *Dream Dare Do. Managing the Most Difficult Person on Earth: Yourself*. Soest: Tyler Roland Press.

Tucker, A., and A. Edmondson. December 2002. "Why Hospitals Don't Learn from Failures: Organizational and Psychological. Dynamics That Inhibit System Change." *California Management Review* 45, no. 2, pp. 55–72.

Womack, J., D. Jones, and D. Roos. 1990. *The Machine that Changed the World. The Story of Lean Production - Toyota's Secret Weapon In The Global Car Wars That Is Now Revolutionizing World Industry*. New York, NY: Simon & Schuster.

About the Author

Because of his training as an engineer Arnout's focus in the first years of his working life was on production and project management. For example, he made an effort to be a manager and improve processes in the automotive industry. His passion lies in working environments with high logistical complexity. A little later he noticed his preference for working with people and systems and the indispensable connection between them.

Lean Principles

His career took a turn toward consultancy at an agency where the main focus was on substantive collaboration. Focused on the work floor and creating very innovative ideas. He became acquainted with the challenging principle of "zero defect": the ultimate pursuit of perfection. He also learned and experienced what was needed for world-class performance—making people aware of their responsibility for their own performance and the continuous possibilities for improvement and supporting that with a system of appropriate tools, coaching, and mentoring. In other words, working according to the Lean principles—a clear system that exposes mistakes and waste and that has everything to do with mindset, behavioral change, and leadership.

Transforming Healthcare

It became increasingly clear to him that this way of working was not only reserved for the industry. This transformation could be realized in many more branches! At the same time as a young father he ran into things in healthcare that he thought could be done in a much better way. When at that time he also received a request from the healthcare sector to use his vision in healthcare he started to focus on the transformation in healthcare.

The Improvement Practice

In 2010 together with a business partner he founded his own training and coaching agency De Verbeterpraktijk holding the ambition to achieve "world-class care" through continuous improvements. In the beginning they were true pioneers in the field of care and they could immediately start working as Lean coaches in various leading hospitals such as VUmc and AMC in Amsterdam. Here they taught hundreds of employees—from nurses to doctors and from team leaders to board members—how to keep improving. In addition, they taught them how to coach their colleagues and spread Lean further. He also assisted various doctors who needed advice on how to start improving complex care processes.

The Lean Mentor: Coaching Coaches

Meanwhile he is more and more often working as a mentor in one-on-one contacts. His focus is on difficult leadership and change issues in healthcare for which a broad Lean experience is desirable. He mainly helps people who already have experience in improving and innovating healthcare, including healthcare professionals, their managers, and Lean coaches.

No One Wants to Return to the Old Style

His experience so far is that everyone he coaches and who works according to Lean principles in the way he advocates never wants to return to the old style. Experience it for yourself and grant yourself and others the transformation to the best possible care there is.

Arnout as Author

Based on all his experiences with Lean transformations in healthcare he wrote *Lean Thinking in Healthcare: Safe, Compassionate, Zero Waste, No Struggle* (Orelio 2019, in Dutch; Orelio 2021, in English), an overview work with which he hopes to reach everyone in healthcare who wants to improve. This book, *Lean Thinking for Emerging Healthcare Leaders,* is a spin-off of *Lean Thinking in Healthcare.* It is specifically aimed at healthcare professionals with leadership responsibilities and/or ambitions. It focuses on *how to* apply lean principles, improve processes, and develop yourself and others.

All the tools from Arnout's books can be downloaded from his website: leanthinkinginhealthcare.com. Scan the QR-code. It will take you straight to the *Lean Thinking in Healthcare* tools-page.

Index

OTHER TITLES IN THE HEALTHCARE MANAGEMENT COLLECTION

- *Behind the Scenes of Health Care* by Hesston L. Johnson
- *Process-Oriented Healthcare Management Systems* by Anita Edvinsson
- *Predictive Medicine* by Emmanuel Fombu
- *The DNA of Physician Leadership* by Myron J. Beard and Steve Quach

Concise and Applied Business Books

The Collection listed above is one of 30 business subject collections that Business Expert Press has grown to make BEP a premiere publisher of print and digital books. Our concise and applied books are for...

- Professionals and Practitioners
- Faculty who adopt our books for courses
- Librarians who know that BEP's Digital Libraries are a unique way to offer students ebooks to download, not restricted with any digital rights management
- Executive Training Course Leaders
- Business Seminar Organizers

Business Expert Press books are for anyone who needs to dig deeper on business ideas, goals, and solutions to everyday problems. Whether one print book, one ebook, or buying a digital library of 110 ebooks, we remain the affordable and smart way to be business smart. For more information, please visit www.businessexpertpress.com, or contact sales@businessexpertpress.com.

Printed in the USA
CPSIA information can be obtained
at www.ICGtesting.com
LVHW010305230823
755964LV00002B/169